_anguage to go

ELEMENTARY

TEACHER'S RESOURCE BOOK

Simon le Maistre

with Mark Trussell, Drew Hyde and Kenna Bourke

Series Editor: Simon Greenall

Longman

w.longman.com

Pearson Education Limited
Edinburgh Gate, Harlow
Essex CM20 2JE, England
and Associated Companies throughout the world.

www.language-to-go.com

Language to go is a trademark of Pearson Education Limited.

First published 2002.

Set in 10pt Univers Light.

Printed in Spain by Mateu Cromo, S.A. Pinto (Madrid).

ISBN 0 582 40414 2

Publishing acknowledgements

Development Editor and Project Manager: Bernie Hayden
Editors: Fran Banks, Rosemary Morlin, Catriona Watson-Brown.
We would like to thank Dorothy Rippon for her invaluable
comments on the Photocopiable activities.

Designed by Gemini Design.

Cover design by Juice Creative.

Series design by Steve Pitcher.

The photographs of the authors on page 10/back cover by
James Walker.
Illustrated by: Jeff Anderson, David Cuzik, Alan Fraser and
Bob Harvey (Pennant Inc.), Gary Andrews, Kes Hankin and
Mark Vallance (Gemini Design).

We are grateful to the following for permission to reproduce
copyright photographs:
Getty Images/FPG International/Doug Corrance for 77 (top left,
bottom right); Peter Gridley for 111 (middle left);
Getty Images/Stone/Oliver Benn for 77 (top right, bottom left);
Ronald Grant Archive for 121 (top left, bottom left); © Rosemary
Morlin for 111 (top left).

Front cover photographs left to right: Powerstock Zefa;
Corbis Stock Market; Image State; Photo Disc.

Contents

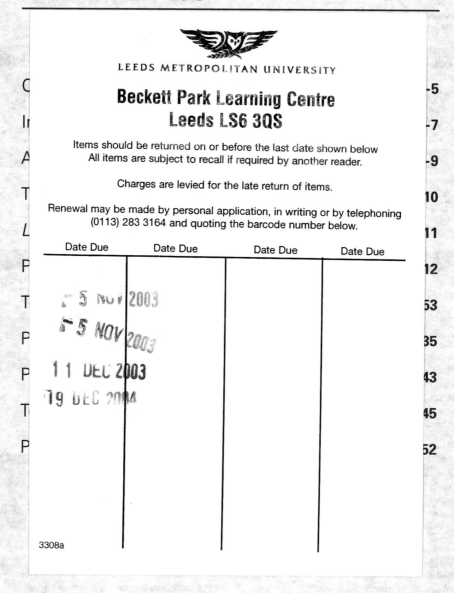

Contents map of Students' Book

Introduction

About *Language to go*

Many adult students of English have a limited amount of time for their studies. They may require English for both professional and social reasons, and are also aware that they're likely to use it in a number of international situations. They need to ensure that the time they spend on their English learning is highly focused and goal oriented. They need to be able to achieve certain tasks and to leave a language class, sometimes after a busy and tiring day of working or studying, with a bite-sized chunk of *Language to go* and a sense of 'Yes, I can do that – anywhere in the world, in English!'

Language to go is a short course for this kind of adult student. Our underlying principle is that students start the class with an objective defined in terms of a realistic outcome, and finish with the language they need to achieve it. So here's a quick overview of what the course contains:

- Four levels: Elementary, Pre-Intermediate, Intermediate and Upper Intermediate. Each level has 40 teaching lessons, and each lesson has been carefully written so that it takes around 60 minutes in the classroom.
- A Practice section, a Grammar reference and the recording scripts at the back of the Students' Book.
- A detachable Phrasebook in the Students' Book.
- A class cassette or CD with the listening material.
- This Teacher's Resource Book, containing a step-by-step guide to every lesson (including answer keys), photocopiable activities, photocopiable tests and a Writing bank.
- The *Language to go* website (www.language-to-go.com).

Language to go – a closer look

Students' Book

Content

Each teaching lesson is designed to last 60 minutes and is contained on two facing pages, which reinforces visually the relationship between the Students' Book lesson and the classroom lesson. It focuses on a final activity, by presenting and practising the language required and then inviting students to perform the activity at the end of the lesson. The lesson begins with a presentation of the vocabulary needed for the final activity, then continues with reading or listening material which presents the target structure(s) in a meaningful context. This is followed by some inductive grammar work, focusing on the meaning and the form of the structure, and by some practice exercises. Students should now be equipped to do the final activity in the *Get talking* section at the end of the lesson, which is sometimes accompanied by a *Get writing* section. The *Language to go* is exemplified in an easily memorised dialogue in the bottom corner of each right-hand page and acts as the focus and goal of the lesson.

Motivation is at the core of successful learning in general, and language learning in particular; we have therefore taken great care to choose topics and texts which will stimulate the student intellectually as well as linguistically. Much of the material has been chosen so that it reflects the international community of English users, as native or non-native speakers.

We have tried to use as many international contexts as possible, since we're aware that our students will use their newly acquired linguistic competence not just in their own country or in an English-speaking one, but all around the world.

Cyclical syllabus

The course design of Pre-Intermediate, Intermediate and Upper Intermediate is based on a **cyclical syllabus**, in which different aspects of language, such as tenses, modals, vocabulary or functions, are presented several times in the same level. The advantage of this approach is that the structures can be naturally revised, recycled and consolidated on a regular and frequent basis. It also allows schools and institutes with a system of continuous enrolment to ensure that students who arrive later in the course are not disadvantaged by missing out on lessons which have already dealt with key structures.

At Elementary level, we have not used a cyclical syllabus, as it does not meet the needs of Elementary students, for whom a specific sequence of acquiring language is more useful. It is also true that this level lends itself less well to courses with continuous enrolment.

The principal **syllabuses** in the course are Grammar and Vocabulary. The approach to grammar is largely one of guided discovery in which the students are presented with examples of the target structure and then invited to work out the rules relating to form and meaning. Much of the vocabulary is presented in chunks as well as individual words, to reflect the way we use English in real life.

Skills
The **skills** of reading, listening, writing and speaking are all practised. Speaking is at the core of the philosophy of *Language to go*, and is the skill most often practised, both in the *Get talking* sections and in the pair and group work activities. The reading and listening material includes examples of English which may be beyond the immediate level of students, but is treated in a way which prepares them for dealing with it in a real-life context. Writing is deliberately not practised extensively, since we feel that it is a skill which can be more usefully developed outside the classroom, allowing the interactive opportunities of the classroom to be exploited to their maximum on a short course. However, several lessons also include a *Get writing* activity, and further guidance is given in the Writing bank in this book.

Pronunciation is dealt with wherever it is appropriate to the grammar or the vocabulary syllabus strands, focusing on stress in words, stress in sentences and intonation patterns rather than individual phonemes.

Additional material
The **Practice section** provides further exercises to consolidate the language taught in the main lesson. For teachers who have classes lasting longer than 60 minutes, it can be used in class, either after the *Practice* exercises or at the end of the main lesson. The exercises in the Practice section can also be set for homework and have been written so that students can work on them alone.

The **Grammar reference** is designed to be a more descriptive explanation of the grammar points covered in the main teaching lesson.

Phrasebook
This is a reformulation of some of the language taught in the course, as well as a reminder of other relevant words and expressions which are appropriate to the level, and presented in a familiar phrasebook style.
A traditional phrasebook, with its list of useful words and expressions, is at the core of the concept of *Language to go*; in other words, language which is organised and can be readily accessed when required in real-life situations.

Teacher's Resource Book
This book contains:
- a lesson-by-lesson contents map;
- this introduction, with an overview of the course;
- some tips on how to make the most of the material;
- a personal statement from the authors;
- how *Language to go* links with external examinations;

- a phonemic chart;
- step-by-step Teaching notes for each lesson including answer keys;
- photocopiable activities;
- photocopiable Tests with answer key;
- photocopiable Writing bank.

Photocopiable activities
Teachers who have more than 60 minutes' class time available may wish to provide further skills practice, so we have provided some extra material. There are 40 extra activities, each one corresponding to a Students' Book lesson, which are designed to be photocopied and distributed to the students. Each activity will provide a further twenty to 30 minutes' practice of the language taught in the lesson. The teaching notes opposite each photocopiable activity are for your reference, providing a guide to how the activity should be organised and answer keys where relevant.

Photocopiable tests and answer keys
These are to be used to check on the students' progress at regular intervals during the course. There are four for each level, and they focus on the vocabulary and grammar covered in every ten lessons. So the ideal time to do these tests will be when you have finished Lessons 10, 20, 30 and 40.

Photocopiable writing bank
This can be used at any point in the course when you think it appropriate for students' needs, or to help guide them with a particular *Get writing* activity.

The *Language to go* website
By clicking onto www.language-to-go.com, you will find material of interest to both students and teachers, including further interactive practice exercises for each lesson. There are also self-study versions of the main Grammar / Language focus of each lesson, and these serve as useful review exercises.

Language to go is an exciting and innovative course of international English. It combines the basic requirements of a tightly focused and minimalist short course with the wealth of materials appropriate to the learning potential of adults in the 21st century.
It contains topics and texts designed to motivate adult students with social and professional reasons for learning English. It has been written with a mixture of enthusiasm, passion and pedagogical rigour by a team of talented authors, and produced by editors, designers, researchers and many others with much love and care. So, now it's over to you with *Language to go*. We hope you and your students enjoy it.

Simon Greenall
Series Editor

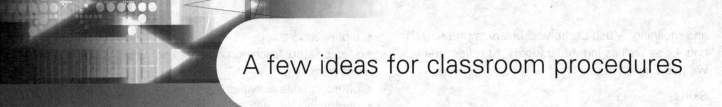

A few ideas for classroom procedures

Personalisation

Most adult students of English are willing to trust their teachers because they believe everything they do is in their best interests. But now and then, they must ask themselves, 'Why am I doing this? How is this relevant to me?' When this happens, both student and teacher are faced with a potential challenge to their motivation.

Personalisation allows students to relate material to their own world. It is therefore a key factor in maintaining their motivation, especially during challenging activities like roleplays. The teacher has to make sure the student understands how an activity relates to their language-learning needs. Every activity in *Language to go* is designed to allow maximum personalisation for students. The lessons are all constructed around a final activity, and these activities will usually provide an opportunity for them to adapt the language being used to their own circumstances. For example, during the presentation of a new topic, there is usually an appeal to the student to think about how much they might know about it. On other occasions, there may be an invitation to use the target vocabulary or grammar in sentences which are relevant to the student.

If you feel that personalisation might be lacking at any stage, for example, after a vocabulary exercise, you could suggest that students choose four or five words which they think might be useful to them, or which look like words in their language, or which sound nice, or which they can place in categories of their own choice. After a grammar activity, encourage students to write a couple of sentences about themselves using the target structure. You don't need to correct these extra activities, although you may want to ask them to share their answers with the rest of the class. In this way, personalisation can have two purposes: to consolidate the learning process and to make what they're doing relevant to themselves.

Vocabulary

The words and expressions which form the focus of the Vocabulary sections are those which we think are important at this level. Most lessons only contain between eight and ten items for productive learning (that is, words which the student should be able to use in spoken or written work, and not words which they are able to recognise).

Many of the vocabulary items are grouped in topics; others are grouped according to some of the rules behind word formation or collocation in English.

Encourage students to keep a vocabulary list containing all the items which they have learnt. Try to ensure that the list categorises the words in different ways, in order to consolidate the learning process.

When students ask for help in understanding words, try not to explain too many immediately, but ask them to help each other, or to use dictionaries if they're available in the classroom. Remember also that explaining new words may build their vocabulary, but it may not develop their ability to work out the meaning of words in reading and listening activities.

Speaking

There are many opportunities for speaking practice in *Language to go*. Firstly, there are many pair and group work activities based on a reading, listening, grammar or vocabulary task. Secondly, there are some lessons which focus on functional language where there is a clear model of the language to be used. Thirdly, most of the final activities in the lesson (*Get talking*) are opportunities to practise speaking. Remember to aim for a balance between accuracy and fluency; not every activity needs your close and careful correction of errors.

Listening

The listening material contains examples of everyday, natural spoken English. Students may be worried by the speed of delivery, thinking that it's too fast, so reassure them that this is also quite normal in real life, and that the classroom is the best place to be exposed to this type of natural language. They don't need to speak as fast themselves, but they do need practice in understanding authentic spoken English. The following guidelines should help them:

- Encourage students to focus on the main ideas of the listening passage and not get distracted by words they don't understand. The main activity will usually help them to do this.
- Help them to interpret clues from the context (situation, tone of voice etc.). This will usually enable them to understand a great deal more than the words will convey.
- Play the recording a couple of times (more than this will start to compromise their motivation), even if the instructions only suggest once.
- Try not to play the recording and stop after every phrase, as this will not give them the important practice in listening to the discourse of spoken English.

Writing

Writing is usually suggested in the *Get writing* sections as a way of showing that students have mastered the language which has been focused on in the lesson. They are all meant to be classroom versions of situations they may encounter outside the classroom – letters, e-mails, exam-style essays etc. The *Writing bank* in this Teacher's Resource Book provides photocopiable models of these writing genres with accompanying suggestions on how to exploit them in class.

Encourage students to practise a form of *process writing*: ask them to write down as much as they can without worrying too much about being accurate. Then ask them to reread what they have written, or maybe even show it to a partner. Encourage them to be critical and to revise their work if necessary. Then ask them to write a final version which incorporates extra ideas and all their corrections. Remember that writing can be an exercise in fluency as well as accuracy.

Reading

Much of the reading material involves words which students may not have come across, just like in real life. Many of the accompanying activities are designed both to support their general understanding of the passage as they read it, and to check their comprehension afterwards.

Try not to answer questions about difficult words, but instead, encourage students to work out the meaning for themselves.

Make sure that students read the passage once, perhaps at the end of the lesson, just to enjoy it, to respond with natural interest to it and without having to answer difficult questions!

Roleplays

The roleplays are presented as a further opportunity for students to practise speaking. Some students enjoy roleplays, especially in a foreign language. Others find they make enormous demands on their imagination. For this reason, we have tried to provide suitable support into the roleplays, so that less imaginative or creative students don't feel under pressure to come up with all the ideas themselves. Go round the pairs or groups as they are doing the roleplays, listening but not interrupting, unless they want help in what they need to do.

Try to avoid correcting students as they are doing their roleplays, but make a note of major mistakes, if you wish, and discuss them with the whole class at the end of the lesson.

Error correction

It's a good idea to think about what and when you correct before the lesson begins. Make this decision part of your lesson plan.

It's best to avoid correction during an activity which focuses on fluency until after it's over; on the other hand, it may be best to correct students in an activity which focuses on accuracy as they do it. Look at each activity in turn, decide what its aim is and choose the best strategy.

Remember that less-confident students will need more encouragement than others, and your correction may compromise their motivation.

You may also decide you only want to indicate the student has made an error rather than correct it yourself. Think carefully about your attitude to error correction, and share your opinions with the whole class.

Jigsaw reading

Some activities involve a technique known as *jigsaw reading*. This involves students working in pairs. The first instruction will be to work separately on a reading passage, with separate but complementary tasks to perform. This usually involves them turning to a specified text or activity in the *Information for pair and group work* section at the back of the Students' Book. The second instruction will be to work together and to share the information they have gathered from the separate tasks.

This technique is at the very heart of communicative language teaching, as it involves an information gap (Student A knows something that Student B doesn't, and vice versa) and a meaningful exchange of information during the second stage of the activity, where the students tell each other what they have learnt.

As long as the students understand the instructions, it's best for the teacher simply to signal the start of the two stages of the activity, and listen as the pairs/groups perform it. You can finish the activity sequence with group feedback to check the answers are correct.

Pronunciation *discussion.*

Pronunciation work in *Language to go* focuses more on word and sentence stress and intonation patterns than on individual phonemes. There are several techniques you can use:

- *Drilling* can be individual or choral repetition of a word or a sentence. Choral repetition with the whole class is a way of building up students' confidence in pronouncing strange words or new sentences.

- *Backchaining* involves the repetition of different parts of a sentence, often starting at the end, and gradually adding parts until you have reconstituted the whole sentence.

- *Word linking* focuses on the fact that when you say words in connected speech, the individual phonemes which make up the word may change. Say the words separately, then say them in connected speech and emphasise the way in which they sound different.

The *Language to go* authors

Simon le Maistre

Simon le Maistre

I am a writer, trainer and teacher with over twelve years' experience in English language teaching worldwide. After graduating from Cambridge, I fell into teaching by accident, but soon found that ELT could offer an exciting and varied career. After five years abroad in Italy and Spain, I returned to the UK to work for International House, London, as a teacher trainer, running courses in the UK, Eastern Europe and South Africa. More recently, I have become interested in online learning and have been working with Pearson Education developing e-learning materials for web-based English language teaching and training.

Language to go Elementary has been a collaborative effort, with over twenty years of combined teaching experience poured into it. It includes those aspects I think are crucial to successful learning: giving students useful, relevant language; giving students thinking time; and giving students real-world communicative tasks for which they are fully prepared. My special interest as a trainer has always involved minimum input from the teacher while getting maximum output from the students, and hopefully that is reflected in the course book. It's clear enough for inexperienced teachers to pick up and go and flexible enough for experienced teachers to use and develop. And all that on two pages!

When not writing, much of my spare time is spent mountain biking, travelling and cooking.

Carina Lewis

Carina Lewis

I am a teacher and teacher trainer at International House, London. I graduated from Oxford Brookes University, where I studied Accountancy and Maths. Having learnt that I did not want to be an accountant, I moved into the field of marketing. With an urge to travel, I decided to do a CELTA course at International House London, which I found to be an excellent learning experience and the start of an unexpected career in ELT.

I have been teaching English for eight years and have worked in Brazil, Poland, Portugal and the UK. I have taught all levels and a range of age groups. I took the RSA DTEFLA course in 1997, and since then have continued teaching and have trained teachers from all parts of the world in both the state and private sector. I have thoroughly enjoyed my career in ELT, and it has offered me varied jobs involving contact with people from all parts of the world, teaching, training, writing and work as Director of Studies.

Fortunately, I was able to teach Elementary students while writing *Language to go* and so was able to trial materials on them and get honest feedback on the interest value of the material. I am always keen to get my students talking, so it was important for me to incorporate into our book realistic spoken tasks which practised the vocabulary and grammar introduced in the lesson. The material is easily accessible on two facing pages and clear to follow, which hopefully will involve minimum lesson preparation time for teachers!

Language to go and EFL exams

The table below shows *general* equivalences between the four levels of *Language to go* and two well-known international examination boards, UCLES (University of Cambridge Local Examinations Syndicate) and Trinity College, in terms of the language taught and the topics covered in the four books.

While *Language to go* is not an examination preparation course, a student who has, for example, completed the Elementary level would have sufficient language to attempt UCLES KET, and start a preparation course for UCLES PET. Examination training is required for all EFL examinations, and we would strongly advise students to follow an examination preparation course. But you will find that some of the exercises in the Students' Book lessons, the Practice section and the photocopiable Tests are similar in format to those found in EFL public examinations.

Note that higher-level exams, such as UCLES CPE and ESOL Grades 11–12, are not covered in this table.

For further information, contact:

UCLES
English as a Foreign Language
1 Hills Road
Cambridge
CB1 2EU
United Kingdom
Tel: +44 (0) 1223 553355
Fax: +44 (0) 1223 460278
E-mail: eflhelpdesk@ucles.org.uk
www.ucles.org.uk

Trinity College
89 Albert Embankment
London
SE1 7TP
United Kingdom
Tel: +44 (0)20 7820 6100
Fax: +44 (0)20 7820 6161
E-mail: info@trinitycollege.co.uk
www.trinitycollege.co.uk

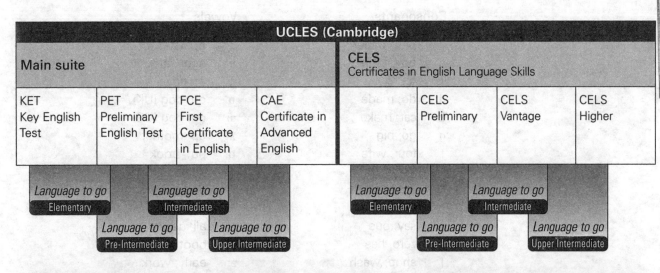

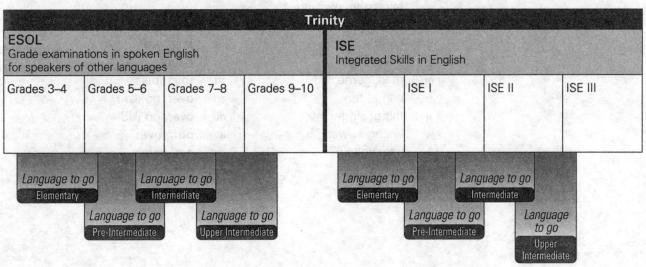

Phonemic symbols

The symbols in this chart represent the sounds used in standard British English and some of the most common variations in American English. We have used the symbols in the Teaching notes to help clarify pronunciation points dealt with in the lesson. We have not included them in the Students' Book, because we feel it is not always easy or practical to teach them on a short course or a course involving continuous enrolment.

However, you may find it useful to introduce certain symbols to students to help them with their individual pronunciation needs. If you do, we would recommend that you:

• only teach a few symbols at a time – little and often;
• get students to practise the sounds, but do not aim for perfection – a comprehensible approximation is good enough;
• relate the symbols to words which students already know.

The example words here are all taken from the Longman defining vocabulary of 2,000 words used in *The Longman Active Study Dictionary* and *The Longman Dictionary of Contemporary English*.

Consonants		Vowels	
p	pen; paper	ɪ	it; sister
b	boy; table	e	egg; said
t	to; sit	æ	at; have
d	do; made	ɒ	on; dog (UK)
k	car; make	ɒː	on; dog (US)
g	go; big	ʌ	up; mother
f	four; wife	ʊ	put; book
v	very; live	ə	address; brother
θ	think; tooth	iː	easy; she
ð	this; other	ɑː	art; father
s	say; bus	ɔː	all; door
z	zero; has	uː	boot; shoe
ʃ	shop; wash	ɜː	early; work
ʒ	television; pleasure		
h	have; ahead	**Diphthongs**	
tʃ	cheese; watch	eɪ	able; wait
dʒ	job; bridge	aɪ	I; buy
m	man; come	ɔɪ	toy; noise
n	name; ten	əʊ	over; go (UK)
ŋ	thing; singer	oʊ	over; go (US)
w	water; flower	aʊ	out; town
l	late; yellow	ɪə	ear; here
r	run; carry	eə	air; there (UK)
j	yes; you	ʊə	sure; poor

Teaching notes

by Simon le Maistre

Vocabulary	Personal information
Function	Greetings
Grammar	*To be: am, is, are*
Language to go	Introducing yourself

Meeting people

Language notes

- Note the contracted forms of *be*: *I am = I'm, he is = he's, you are = you're, we are = we're, they are = they're*. Contractions are extremely common in everyday informal English, and are presented throughout the book as the 'main' option.
- *Hello* and *goodbye* are both formal and informal; *hi* and *bye* are informal.
- Countries have capital letters e.g. *Brazil* not ~~brazil~~.
- Students often omit the definite article when talking about *the USA*. For most countries the definite article is omitted (*France, Italy*) but not for *the USA* and *the UK*.

Way in

- Greet students. Say 'My name's ….' and ask 'What's your name?' Elicit the response 'My name's ….'. Practise the question around the class. Next, students ask and answer across the room in open pairs and then in closed pairs.
- They then stand up and mingle, asking and answering around the class.

Vocabulary

1 Ask students to look at the picture. Ask 'Where is it?' and elicit 'In an Internet café.'
   - Point out the example answers and students then work in pairs to complete the chat room form with the vocabulary in the box.

Jobs: doctor; student; businessman/woman
Marital status: single; married
Country: Poland; the USA; Brazil
Interests: learning English; films; music; sport

Reading

2 Show students the first e-mail and ask the whole class 'Which e-mail is number 2?'.
   - Students then work in pairs to complete the activity.
   - Note that *on 5th Street* is US English. In UK English *in* is used, for example, *in Market Street/London Road*.

Correct order:
1 Hi. My name's Vanessa …
2 Hello, Vanessa. My name's …
3 Hi Marek …
4 Hello again, Vanessa …

3 Students find the photo of Marek and Vanessa on page 89. Make sure they realise that even though Marek and Vanessa are communicating by e-mail, they are in the same Internet café in San Francisco.
   - Point out the way they introduce themselves with *Nice to meet you. And you*. This is how people greet each other the first time they meet.

They're in an Internet café.

Language focus

4 Ask the students to work in pairs and write the responses to the greetings. Don't check the correct answers with the students yet.

1 Hi.   2 Fine, thanks.   3 Bye.

5a 🔲 Play the recording for students to listen and check their answers to Exercise 4.

5b 🔲 Play the conversation again. Stop the recording after the first greeting and get the students to repeat it chorally. Ask individual students to repeat it and check their pronunciation. Play the response, stop the recording and repeat the process.
   - Follow this procedure with the rest of the conversations.

Practice

6 Divide the students into pairs. Practise the greetings and replies across the class in open pairs to check students are confident with the language before asking them to practise in closed pairs.
   - Alternatively, students stand up and practise around the class in a mingling activity.

Grammar focus

7 Students read the example sentences and rules about the verb *be*. Focus on the difference between the contractions and the full form in the table.

8 🔲 Play the recording and stop it after the first sentence for students to repeat as a class. Ask individuals to repeat it to check their pronunciation.
   - Repeat this process with the other sentences.

Practice

9 Students put the correct form of *be* into the gaps. Check students know the full form and the contractions and accept either as correct.

1 'm/am   2 'm/am   3 're/are   4 's/is   5 's/is
6 're/are

10 Write an example e-mail on the board about you. *My name's … and I'm a teacher …* Students then write an e-mail about themselves.
   - Go round and correct/help with grammar and vocabulary, especially for jobs and countries, which might be relevant to the students but different to the ones covered in the lesson.

Get talking

11 Ask the students to stand up and mingle and introduce themselves. Explain that they must use the information from the e-mail they wrote and find a student who they want to write an e-mail to. Encourage the students to use the greetings and responses from the Language focus.
   - If students already know each other, they should find a student who has similar interests to them to write e-mails to.

Vocabulary Everyday objects
Grammar Plurals; *What is/are …?*
Language to go Asking and answering: personal information

Personal details, please!

Language notes

- Students often have problems with contractions. The contraction *what's = what is*. *What are* is not usually contracted when written, but it often sounds contracted when spoken.
- Note the weak pronunciation of *your* /jə/ in questions like *What's your name?*
- Note the US English equivalents of *mobile phone* and *postcode* are *cellphone* and *zipcode*.

Way in

- Bring in three or four of the objects shown in the catalogue and ask 'What's this in English?' Elicit / Teach the word and check students' pronunciation.

Vocabulary

1   Point out the example to students, and do another with them if you feel it necessary.

> 1 battery   2 watch   3 camera   4 mobile phone
> 5 laptop   6 bag   7 calculator   8 dictionary
> 9 briefcase   10 wallet   11 pen   12 diary   13 notebook

2   ▭ Write *battery* on the board and play the example on the recording. Then say the word with different stresses to elicit the correct one and mark the stress on the word with a square.
- Students listen to the recording and write the stress on the correct syllable of the words in the box. You could stop the recording after the first one to check students have the correct answer before playing the recording to the end.

> battery   watch   camera   mobile phone   laptop
> bag   calculator   dictionary   briefcase   wallet
> pen   diary   notebook

Grammar focus

3   Students read the examples and write the plural form of the words in the table. Point out how the plural can end in *-s*, *-ies* or *-es*.

> Plural: wallets; watches; dictionaries; pens; batteries; briefcases

Listening

4   ▭ Students are going to listen to a phone conversation between a customer and a telesales assistant. Check they know the meaning of the words on the left of the form.
Explain that students need to tick the correct information on the form (not all is correct).
- Play the recording and stop it after the first answer to check students understand the activity. Then play the recording through to the end.

> Surname ✓   Initials ✗   Address ✓   Postcode ✓
> Presents ✗   Credit card number ✓   Job ✗
> E-mail address ✓

5   Students listen again and correct the wrong information on the form.
- Students can compare their answers in pairs, and listen again if necessary, before checking the answers with the whole class.
- Note that in the UK, the *postcode* gives you information about the town / city, the street and the house. In US English, *postcode* is referred to as *zipcode*.

> Initials: T P
> Presents: 2 batteries, watch and camera
> Job: a doctor

Grammar focus

6   Students read the example questions and complete the table. Remind students that *what are* is not contracted but sometimes sounds contracted when spoken.

> Singular: *What*'s your credit card number?
> Plural: *What are* they?

7   ▭ Play the recording and ask students to repeat the words chorally after each line. Stop the recording after the final line of the first item and ask individuals to repeat it to check their pronunciation. Then play the second item and repeat the process.

Practice

8   Students write the correct question next to the prompt.

> 1 What's / What is your surname?
> 2 What are your initials?
> 3 What's / What is your e-mail address?
> 4 What's / What is your address?
> 5 What's / What is your postcode?
> 6 What are your work and home phone numbers?
> 7 What are your presents?

Get talking and writing

9   Explain that the students need to choose two presents they would like to buy from the catalogue. Divide the students into pairs, one customer and one telesales assistant. Tell the customer to order the presents and the assistant to write the personal details on the form.
- Students then change roles and repeat the activity.
- For an example of form filling, see **Writing bank** page 146.

Vocabulary   Nationalities and countries
Grammar   *To be* (questions and negatives)
Language to go   Asking about nationalities

Round the world

Language notes

- Note the contractions in the negative of the verb *be*: *isn't* = *is not* and *aren't* = *are not* but we can't say ~~I amn't~~. We must use *I'm not*.
- Students often have problems forming questions and may make questions without the inversion. Common mistakes include: ~~You are Italian?~~ [*Are you Italian?*]
- Note the short answer form *Yes, I am.* and *No, I'm not.* There is no contraction of the short answer form ~~Yes I'm.~~
- Nationalities and countries have capital letters. E.g. *American* not ~~american~~.

Way in

- Bring in three or four objects / pictures associated with different parts of the world, for example a coke can (the USA), pasta (Italy) and ask 'Where's it from?'. Elicit / Give the countries.

Vocabulary and speaking

1 Point out the example and do one or two with the whole class if necessary.

> Japan – Japanese; the USA – American; Russia – Russian; Brazil – Brazilian, Poland – Polish; Turkey – Turkish; the UK – British; France – French

2 Demonstrate the activity by saying a country and asking the students for the corresponding nationality.
- Divide the students into pairs, A and B. Student A tests Student B, who has their book closed. Students change roles and continue to test each other. For variety, ask A to say the nationality and B to say the country.

Reading

3 Students work in pairs and circle the correct answers to the quiz. Don't tell students the correct answers yet.

Listening

4 📖 Play the recording for students to check their answers to Exercise 3.

> Leisure and Entertainment: 1 isn't   2 is   3 aren't
> Food and Drink: 1 b   2 b   3 c
> Famous People: 1 b   2 a   3 b

Extra information: *Tango* is a fast, sensual ballroom dance first developed in Buenos Aires, Argentina, in the 1880s. *Judo* 'gentle way', is a martial art whose aim is to use skill and flexibility to defeat your opponent. *Kendo* 'way of the sword' is the traditional Japanese art of fencing with a wooden sword. *Bigos* is a Polish stew made with meat and cabbage, traditionally simmered for several days before serving. *Gisele Bundchen* is a Brazilian-born international top model. *J K Rowling* is the author of the *Harry Potter* books. She is British and an ex English teacher. *Elton John* is a famous singer, composer and pianist who is one of the most popular entertainers of the 20th century. *George Michael* is a British-born international singer / songwriter.

Grammar focus

5 Students read the example sentences and complete the table. Point out the rules about contractions for negatives, questions and short answers.
Explain that the contraction for *I am not* is *I'm not* (not ~~I amn't~~). Positive short answers are not contracted: *Yes, she is.* (not ~~Yes, she's~~).

> Negatives: He / She / It *isn't* American. We / You / They *aren't* Chinese.
> Questions: *Is* she (he / it) British?
> Short answers: Yes, she *is*. No, she *isn't*.
> Questions: *Are* they (we / you) Chinese?
> Short answers: Yes, they *are*. No, they *aren't*.

Practice

6 Students use the prompts to write correct sentences. Do the first one as an example on the board with the whole class.

> 1 Pizzas aren't Greek. They're Italian.
> 2 He isn't American. He's Canadian.
> 3 Baseball isn't Spanish. It's American.
> 4 You aren't Brazilian. You're Argentinian.
> 5 Seville oranges aren't French. They're Spanish.
> 6 She isn't English. She's Irish.

7 Students write the questions and short answers. Make sure they write a short answer after *Yes*. or *No*.

> 1 A: Is he from Italy? B: Yes, he is.
> 2 A: Are they German? B: Yes, they are.
> 3 A: Is she French? B: No, she isn't.
> 4 A: Are you Polish? B: Yes, I am.
> 5 A: Are they from Brazil? B: Yes, they are.
> 6 A: Is he from Argentina? B: No, he isn't.

Get writing and talking

8 Explain that students are going to write a quiz in the same style as Exercise 3. Divide students into groups (of four) and name each group A or B. Each group then refers to their group's information to write the quiz.
- Students do their quizzes with a new partner from another group.

Extra information:
The earliest version of the game of *chess* probably came from India (6th century). *Samba* and *Bossa Nova* are types of music from Brazil. *Guinness* is a traditional Irish black beer known as *stout*. *Pitta bread* is a type of thin, unleavened bread often used in sandwiches. *Kebabs* are pieces of meat on a stick grilled over a fire. *Astérix* and *Obélix* are fictional French cartoon characters. *André Agassi* is a famous American tennis player and winner of Wimbledon. *Sumo* is a traditional Japanese form of wrestling. *Roulette* is a game of chance played in gambling casinos. *Sauerkraut* is a typically German dish of white cabbage that is often served with smoked meats and sausages. *Cognac* is a brandy and *Champagne* is a sparkling wine from France. *Madonna* is a female American singer/songwriter. *Mick Jagger* is a British rock star and lead singer of the Rolling Stones.

Vocabulary Free time activities
Grammar Possessive adjectives and possessive 's
Language to go Talking about people and favourite things

Favourite things

Language notes

- English possessive adjectives do not agree with the objects they describe so students sometimes confuse *his* and *her*. *His* is for men, *her* is for women, and *its* is for objects.
- Students often say ~~the book of David~~ instead of *David's book*.
- The possessive *'s* is sometimes confused with the contraction *'s* of the verb *be*. For example: *David's favourite book's* Animal Farm. (*David's* = possessive *'s*; *book's* = *book is*)

Way in

- Write examples of famous books, shops, newspapers, magazines, sports and restaurants on the board. You can use local or national examples, or international ones such as:
  books: *Harry Potter*, *Tintin*, any title by popular authors
  shops: *Harrods*, *Macy's*
  newspapers: *Washington Post*, *The Times*, *Le Monde*
  magazines: *Vogue*, *Time*
  sports: *football*, *golf*, *basketball*
  restaurants: *McDonald's*, *Maxime's*, *Planet Hollywood*
  Then ask students to give you another example for each one.

Vocabulary

1 Point to the picture of the market and ask 'What's this in English?' Students then complete the activity in pairs.

   a market ✓ (1)   a shop ✓ (3)   a newspaper ✓ (2)
   a restaurant ✓ (5)   a magazine ✓ (4)

2 Do an example with the whole class before students complete the table with the correct words.
   - It is important to introduce students to verb + noun combinations as in *read a book/newspaper/a magazine*. They are used throughout this course to help expand the students' active vocabulary.

   To read: a newspaper; a magazine; a book
   To go to: a market; a shop; a restaurant; a museum
   To watch: a film; a TV programme; a sport

Listening

3 📟 Explain that each of the people in the photos speaks about favourite things. Play the recording for students to match each speaker to a picture.

   Margarita 5   David 2   Min 3   José 1

Grammar focus

4 Students read the sentences and complete the table.
   - Students are sometimes confused by the possessive *'s* and the contracted *'s* in the verb *be*. If this is a problem, write some contrasting sentences on the board and ask students to say whether each sentence contains a possessive *'s* or the verb *be*.
   for example:
   This is Sue's book.
   Sue's American.
   John's interested in music.
   John's watch is Japanese.
   Anna's from Italy.
   Anna's favourite film is Titanic.

   she – her; it – its; we – our; they – their; Maria – Maria's

5 Students work in pairs and complete the rules about *his*, *her* and *their*.

   Use *their* for two or more people or things.
   Use *her* for a woman.
   Use *his* for a man.

Practice

6 Point out the example and do another one with the whole class if necessary.

   1 My   2 my   3 Her   4 Our   5 our   6 His
   7 Sue's   8 your   9 their

Get talking

7 Students complete the first column with five more 'favourites' from Exercise 1 and tick the ones they like in the 'Me' column. Divide students into groups (of three) to interview each other and complete the table. During feedback, nominate a student to tell the class about their partners' favourites, based on the information from the questionnaire.

Vocabulary Activities: verbs and nouns
Grammar Present simple (positive)
Language to go Talking about family occasions

Celebrations

Language notes

- Students often omit the third person -s in the present simple. Encourage students to correct their own errors.
- Students often have problems with the three different pronunciations of the third person -s: /s/ /z/ /ɪz/. (See the phonemic chart on page 12.)
- Although it is irregular, *have/has* is also introduced here because it is a high frequency verb.

Way in

- Write the dates of important celebrations on the board and elicit/give the names of the celebrations. This can be done in English or in the students' own language.
- Common international celebrations are 14 February (Valentine's Day), 4 July (Independence Day, USA), 14 July (Bastille Day/France), 17 March (St Patrick's Day, Ireland). Check the meaning of *celebration* and *celebrate* before asking students how they celebrate one of the dates on the board.

Vocabulary and speaking

1 Point to the photos and elicit the countries and the celebrations.

> 1 A family Thanksgiving dinner in the USA.
> 2 A temple in Japan on New Year's Day.
> 3 Carnival (Notting Hill Carnival, London)

2 Students work in pairs. Point out the example and do another one with the whole class if necessary.

> 1 f   2 g   3 d   4 b   5 h   6 c   7 e   8 i   9 a

3 Students use the expressions to describe Picture 1 as a whole class activity before working in pairs to talk about the other two pictures.

> **Extra information:** *Thanksgiving* is a national holiday in the USA, which takes place annually on the fourth Thursday of November. Families get together for a traditional meal of turkey and pumpkin pie. *Shogatsu* or *New Year's Day* is the most important holiday in Japan. House entrances are decorated, no housework is done and it is traditional to visit a temple. Children are often given money and it is common to visit friends and relatives. Special food is eaten called *osechi ryori*. *Carnival* is a 4-day celebration which usually takes place in February or March, for example, the famous carnivals in Rio de Janeiro and Venice. The UK's biggest carnival is in Notting Hill, London, and takes place at the end of August.

Reading

4 Ask students to check their answers to Exercise 4 in pairs before whole class feedback. This gives you the opportunity to see how much they have understood.

> 1 My mother cooks lunch.   2 I get up at ten o'clock.
> 3 We have lunch at one o'clock.   4 My mother goes for a walk.   5 My father watches football on television.

Grammar focus

5 Students read the examples and complete the rules. Highlight the third person -s and the spelling rules by using colours on the board to make the third person -s more memorable. Also highlight the irregular form of *have/has*.

> 1 We add -s to the verb with *he/she/it* in the present simple positive.
>   Example: eat – eats; cook – *cooks*; play – *plays*
> 2 Example: do – does; go – *goes*; watch – *watches*

Practice

6a Explain the difference between voiced and unvoiced sounds by asking students to put their thumb and forefinger either side of their throat.
- Students say *s* then *z* and they should notice their throat/fingers vibrating slightly with the *z* or voiced sound. Play the recording and students repeat the words chorally. Stop the tape after each word and ask individuals to repeat it and check their pronunciation.

6b Draw the table on the board and play the next part of the recording. Stop it after the first word and write the verb in the correct pronunciation column. Play the recording to the end while students complete the table.

> visit**s**: drinks; eats; gets
> go**es**: gives; plays
> watch**es**: dances

7 Students work in pairs. Point out the example and do another one with the whole class if necessary.

> 1 goes   2 visit   3 cooks   4 drinks   5 eat
> 6 watches   7 give   8 play

8 Divide the students into two groups, A and B. Group A completes the sentences about Rami and Group B about Charlene. Check that both groups have the correct answers. Students then say their information to a new partner from a different group.

> Rami: get up; eat; cooks; drink
> Charlene: get up; eat; drinks; listen
>
> **Extra information:** *Eid Al-Adha* or 'celebration of sacrifice' takes place on the tenth day of the last month of the Islamic calendar. Muslims celebrate by going to their mosque before visiting friends to share a festive meal (usually a sheep). *Jamaican Independence Day* is a national holiday falling on the first Monday in August.

Get talking ...

9 Give students a couple of minutes thinking time to prepare what to say about their special/typical day. Students then work in pairs to talk about their days.

... and writing

10 Show students Amy's letter to Fumino as a model to base their letter on.
- For an example of an informal letter see **Writing bank** page 147.

Vocabulary   Activities: verbs and nouns
Grammar   Present simple (questions and negatives)
Language to go   Talking about ways of communicating

The modern world

Language notes

- Students often have difficulties with the auxiliary verb *do/does* to make negatives and questions.
  Many students omit it and common mistakes include:
  She ~~uses not~~ the Internet. [*doesn't use*]
  She ~~uses~~ the Internet? [*Does she use*]
- Students sometimes omit the auxiliary in the short answer, saying *Yes.* instead of *Yes, I do.*
- Note the contractions *don't = do not, doesn't = does not*
- The pronunciation of *do you* is /djuː/.

Way in

- Ask 'Do you have a phone? A mobile phone? A laptop? A computer?' Find out from a quick show of hands how many in the class use a mobile phone or the Internet every day.

Vocabulary and speaking

1 Do this exercise as a whole class activity.

> 1 C   2 B   3 A

2 Students work in pairs to ask and answer the question.

3 Point out the example and do another one with the whole class if necessary.
- Students have to complete the questions in the questionnaire with the verbs in the box. Present simple questions are new to them. If they ask what *do* means explain that in English you use *do* to make a question.
- If students are interested, let them do the questionnaire individually but do not discuss it or do it in pairs until later (see Exercise 9).

> 1 use   2 buy   3 have   4 book   5 contact   6 listen
> 7 meet   8 do

Listening

4 Play the recording. Students check their answers to Exercise 4 in pairs before whole class feedback.

> Pictures A and B

5 Play the recording a second time. Again, students check their answers in pairs before whole class feedback.

> 1 68%   2 98%   3 70%   4 65%

- If the students are interested, you could play the recording a third time so that students can hear the correct answers in context. At this level, listening can be quite a stressful experience and this activity takes the pressure off whilst giving students vital exposure to the language.

Grammar focus

6 Students read the examples and complete the rules. Highlight the contractions, the use of *do* in the short answers and the word order changes.
- Alternatively, write *You use the Internet.* on the board and underneath write *Do you use the Internet?* to highlight the use of the auxiliary.

> **Negatives**
> I (You/We/They) *don't* buy books online.
> He (She/It) *doesn't* meet people on the Internet.
> **Questions**
> *Do* you use the Internet?
> Yes, I do./No, I don't.
> *Does* she have a bank account?
> Yes, she does./No, she doesn't.

7 Play the recording and stop it after the first item: *Do you.* Students repeat the model as a class and then individually to check their pronunciation. Repeat this process with the other phrases.

Practice

8 Point out the example and do another one with the whole class if necessary.

> 1 Do they study German; don't study
> 2 does she listen to music?; doesn't listen
> 3 Do you use the Internet?; don't use
> 4 do you meet new people?; don't meet
> 5 Does he have a bank account?; doesn't have
> 6 do you contact friends?; don't contact

Get talking

9 Divide students into pairs, A and B. Explain that students must interview each other using the questionnaire on page 14 of their coursebook. Make sure students answering the questions have their books closed to encourage them to really listen to their partner. If the class is weak, then students can do the activity with their books open.
- When students have completed the questionnaire in pairs hold whole class feedback, asking individuals what kind of person they are or their partner is. Encourage students to correct themselves if they omit the third person *-s* when talking about their partner.

Vocabulary   Objects you take on holiday; means of transport
Grammar   *A/an, some/any*
Language to go   Saying what you take on holiday and how you travel

Travelling

Language notes

- *Any* is a determiner used in negatives and questions. Although it has other uses, leave these to a later stage to avoid overloading students at this level.
- Students often have problems with the weak pronunciation of *a/an, some* and *any* in connected speech.
  I've got an /ən/ alarm clock.
  I always take a /ə/ map.
  I've got some /səm/ books.
  Have you got any /əni/ sunglasses?

Way in

- Take in a couple of the items, for example sunglasses, guide books, credit card. Elicit the words and why you might need them. Explain that you are going on holiday and brainstorm things you need. Alternatively students could guess where/what type of holiday you are going on from the objects you have.

Vocabulary and speaking

1 Point out the example and do one or two with the whole class if necessary before students complete the activity in pairs.

> 1 towel   2 swimming trunks   3 books to read
> 4 personal stereo   5 sweaters   6 walking boots
> 7 camera   8 CDs   9 phrasebook   10 guide book
> 11 map   12 film   13 sunglasses   14 credit card
> 15 alarm clock   16 umbrella   17 travellers' cheques

2 Students work in pairs to ask and answer the questions. Tell them not to read the text yet, but to look at the photo of Tim Hall.
- For question 2, ask students to tick items on the list of things to take away on holiday and to put a cross next to two items they think Tim wouldn't take.
- This activity is designed to get students predicting the content and language in the text as well as give them a reason to read the text.

Reading and vocabulary

3 Students read the text and see if their predictions were correct.

> He takes: a camera, a credit card, an alarm clock, some sweaters, some books.
> He doesn't take: a personal stereo, any guide books.

4 Students write the correct preposition to finish the sentences.

> *by* plane; *by* train; *by* bus

5 Point out the pictures of means of transport and ask students to do Exercise 5 individually.

> bus ✗   tram ✓   train ✗   bicycle ✓   car ✓   plane ✓
> boat ✓   taxi ✗   underground/subway ✓

6 Students ask and answer the questions in pairs.

Grammar focus

7 Students read the examples and complete the rules. Highlight the difference between *a* and *an*. You could hold up some of the objects you brought in for the *Way in* and elicit *a/an/some* to check the students have understood.

> We use *a* or *an* when we talk about one thing (singular). We use *some* when we talk about more than one thing (plural), but the number is not important. We use *any* with plural negatives and questions.

- Explain to students that we use *an* before words beginning with a vowel sound (*an alarm clock, an ice cream, an umbrella*) but we use *a* if it is not a vowel sound (*a car, a university*).

8 [□□] Play the recording and stop it after the first expression. Students repeat the model as a class. Then nominate individual students to repeat it and check their pronunciation.
- Repeat this process with the other phrases.

Practice

9 Point out the example. Depending on your class, you could do this activity in pairs or individually.
- Feedback would also be a good opportunity to correct any pronunciation problems you hear.

> 1 an   2 some   3 any   4 any   5 some   6 an
> 7 a   8 some

Get talking

10 Elicit the three different types of holiday in the pictures: beach, safari, city/sightseeing.
- Explain that students need to choose five things to take on the different holidays. Give them a few minutes to prepare their ideas. Students then discuss their five choices for each holiday with their partner but they must both agree on the same five. During feedback, nominate pairs to tell the class about their choices. If the students are interested in the topic, organise a simple class discussion.
- Ask some general questions about the places in the pictures to elicit vocabulary students will need. Ask how people travel on safari and teach *4x4*. Explain that the picture of London shows *'The London Eye'*, a giant wheel from which you get views of the whole city.

Vocabulary	Objects that people collect
Functions	*Have got*
Language to go	Talking about possessions

The collectors

Language notes

- *Have* and *have got* have the same meaning when referring to possession. However, *have got* cannot be used to express a habitual action, for example: ~~*I've got*~~ lunch at twelve every day. [*I have*]
- Students often have problems because *have got* has a different form to *have*. *Have got* does not use the auxiliary *do* or *does* in questions and negatives.
- Note the contracted forms: *'s got = has got*, *'ve got = have got*, *haven't = have not*, *hasn't = has not*. Students sometimes confuse *he's got* with the contraction of the verb *be* (*he's*).
- Students often don't invert the verb when making questions. Students also omit the auxiliary in the short answer. Common mistakes include: ~~*You've got*~~ a collection of books? [*Have you got*] *Yes, ~~I've~~.* [*I have.*]

Way in

- Take in a bag containing everyday objects like a pen, diary, stamps, a toy, a mug, postcards etc. Ideally these would be objects that you could also collect (as a collector). Students guess what objects you have in your bag.

Vocabulary and speaking

1   Check the meaning of *collect* before dividing the students into pairs to make lists.
- Hold whole class feedback to see how many different ideas for 'things people collect' students have thought of.
- Garfield is a popular newspaper cartoon strip about the adventures of a cat. If students are interested, you could brainstorm other comic strip characters, for example, Snoopy and Charlie Brown or Fred Basset.

2   Do an example with the whole class first. Students then do this orally in pairs before whole class feedback. Point to the objects in the picture and elicit the vocabulary.

T-shirt ✓ toy ✓ poster ✓ photo album ✗	
postcard ✗ plate ✓ mug ✗ picture ✓ ornament ✓	

Reading

3   Point out the example. Students read the text and check their answers in pairs before whole class feedback.

1 Garfield 2 Mike and Gayle 3 Jim Davis		
4 220 million		

Grammar focus

4   Students read the examples and complete the tables. Highlight the contractions and the omission of the auxiliary *do* in the questions and negatives.
- Alternatively, write *He has got 3,000 souvenirs.* on the board and underneath write *Has he got 3,000 souvenirs?* to highlight the inversion when making questions.

Positive
I/You/We/They've got 3,000 souvenirs.
He/She/It*'s* got a toy.
Negative
I/You/We/They *haven't* got any toys.
He/She/It *hasn't* got a cat.
Questions
Have you *got* any toys?
Yes, I have.
No, I haven't.
Has she *got* any toys?
Yes, she has.
No, she hasn't.

Practice

5   📟 Play the recording and stop it after the first sentence. Students repeat the model chorally. Then nominate individual students to repeat and check their pronunciation.
- Repeat this process with the other sentences.

6   Students do this activity in pairs. Point out the example and do another one with the whole class if necessary.
- When you check the answers with the whole class make sure everyone understands the contracted forms in Question 6. Write the full forms on the board: *She's got = She has got* and *She's = She is*. Write another contrasting pair of sentences and ask which means *has* and which means *is*, for example: *He's a collector.* (*is*) *He's got a collection of comics.* (*has*)

1 Have you got	2 I've	3 I have	4 haven't
5 Have you	6 She's got	7 haven't	8 He's

Get talking

7   Explain that students are going to interview each other about what they collect.
- Give students a few minutes to complete the questionnaire about themselves before they ask and answer questions about their collections in pairs. If they want, students can add the information about their partner to the questionnaire.
- Encourage some whole class feedback, so that students can find out if anyone in the class has an interesting or unusual collection.

Vocabulary Sports
Grammar Verbs + -*ing*
Language to go Talking about sports you like/hate

Top sports

Language notes

- Students often make mistakes with the verb + -*ing* structure, by omitting the -*ing* or inserting *to* between the two verbs. For example:
  I like play tennis. [*playing*]
  I like to doing karate.
- Note the different spellings of the -*ing* form, for example: *walk – walking, jog – jogging, cycle – cycling*.

Way in

- Draw the Olympic rings on the board and brainstorm the names of as many sports as possible.
- Alternatively, write the names of well-known international/national sports stars and elicit the sport they are famous for.

Vocabulary and speaking

1 Point out the example and do another one (using *play*) with the whole class if necessary. Students then complete the activity in pairs.

   Go: skiing; jogging; walking; cycling; swimming
   Play: tennis; basketball; volleyball; football; golf
   Do: aerobics; karate

2 Students work in pairs to talk about the pictures and name the sports.

   1 aerobics   2 jogging   3 basketball   4 karate
   5 swimming   6 cycling

3 Do this as a whole class activity. Ask students which sports they do and supply the names of other relevant sports if necessary.

Listening

4 Students work in pairs and predict which sports correspond to the statistics shown on the chart. Have whole class feedback on the students' predictions before the students listen to the recording.

5 🔲 Play the recording for students to listen and check their predictions.
   - You may need to play the recording more than once for students to check all their answers.

   basketball 17%; aerobics 21%; jogging 33%;
   cycling 55%; swimming 57%; walking 86%

6 Students read the sentences before listening to the recording again. This will give them time to predict the answers and help support them when they listen to the language in context.

   1 hate   2 like   3 don't mind   4 love   5 don't like
   6 love

Grammar focus

7a Explain the scale moves from dislike (on the left) to like (on the right). Do one verb as an example with the whole class before students complete the activity.

hate   don't like   don't mind   like   love

7b Students then read the examples and complete the rule. Highlight the spelling of verb + -*ing* and the fact that the verbs can also be followed by nouns.
   - Alternatively, write the two sentences on the board and highlight the noun and the verb + -*ing* before students complete the rule.

   The verbs *hate*, *love*, *like* and *don't mind* are followed by a **noun** or a **verb** + -*ing*

   - To reinforce the pattern of the two structures in the examples, call out the names of sports and ask students to give you two ways of expressing the same idea. For example, if you call out *love* and *karate*, the responses are *I love karate.* and *I love doing karate.*

Practice

8 Students can do this activity in pairs. Point out the example and do another one with the whole class if necessary.

   1 loves playing golf; likes walking   2 hate jogging;
   3 hate doing; don't like playing football   4 like doing
   aerobics   5 like skiing; loves it

Get talking

9 Explain that students are going to interview each other about the most popular sports in the class.
   - Students write the names of five more sports on the list. Demonstrate the interview by asking a student 'Do you like swimming?' and explain the points system (one tally mark for each person who *likes* a sport). Students then stand up, mingle and interview each other. At the end they can count up which sport has scored the most points and is the most popular.
   - During whole class feedback, nominate students to tell the class about the most popular sports using the information from their survey.

Vocabulary   Clothes
Function   Asking for information in a shop
Language to go   Shopping for clothes

Shopping

Language notes

- Students often have problems trying to understand every word in a functional exponent. Use mime and gesture to convey the meaning of whole expressions like *Can I try it on?* and *How much is it?* rather than explaining the meaning of each word.
- *This* and *these* are introduced without being focused on. If they cause a problem, point out that *this* is singular and *these* plural. Use mime to highlight the difference between *that* and *those*, pointing at things farther away from you.
- Students often sound 'flat' when using the shopping language. This can come across as rude so encourage students to exaggerate their intonation to sound polite.
- The following words sometimes cause problems. Students often use *is* with plural nouns, such as *trousers*, *clothes* and *trainers*. Students sometimes confuse *shirt* and *skirt*. Students often need help with the pronunciation of *suit* /suːt/ and *sweater* /swetə/.

Way in

- Point to your clothes and elicit the names of clothes and colours. Ask students to guess how much they cost and where you bought them from.
- Quickly practise colours by pointing at objects or items of clothing and getting students to call out the colour.

Vocabulary and speaking

1   Students ask and answer the questions in pairs. Have feedback from the whole class.

2   Point out the example and do another one with the whole class if necessary. Students can finish the activity in pairs.

1 coat	2 sweater	3 skirt	4 boots	5 shirt
6 suit	7 trousers	8 shoes	9 jacket	10 T-shirt
11 shorts	12 trainers			

3   Do this as a whole class activity.
- Explain that the size conversion table shows how sizes are labelled in the UK, the USA and Europe. It shows the sizes for women's suits and dresses and men's suits and coats.
- Elicit from the class which column shows the smallest size and which the largest. Students write the headings in the table.

Table headings (left to right): small; medium; large

Listening

4   ▭▭ Play the recording and stop it after the customer's first question to check students understand the activity. Then play the recording until the end. If students are having problems, play the recording a second time.

1 large	2 trousers	3 red	4 £1,000

Language focus

5   Students work in pairs to complete the table. Point out *this* and *these*.

Table headings (top to bottom):
size
price
colour
other

- Point out the note about the shop assistant's responses. Ask students for which questions in the table they could be responses.

Practice

6   Do the first one as an example with the whole class. Then students work in pairs to complete the activity.
- Check the answers with the whole class to make sure that the completed sentences are correct.

1 Can I help you?
2 Have you got this suit in large?
3 Here you are.
4 Can I try it on?
5 What colour do you like?
6 Have you got this bag in brown?
7 No, sorry.
8 How much are these pens?
9 Have you got this coat in medium?
10 How much is this diary?

7   ▭▭ Play the recording and stop it after the first question. Students repeat the model as a class. Nominate individual students to repeat it and check their pronunciation.
- Repeat this process with the other questions.

8   Divide the students into pairs to practise the dialogue. Demonstrate the activity with a student to show they only need to choose one of the alternatives in the prompt boxes.
- Go round the class, monitoring students' use of language, while they are practising the dialogue. If there are common errors, hold a short feedback session after the activity.
- After finishing a dialogue, students change roles.

Get talking

9   Divide students into A and B and check they know the objects in their respective pictures. Encourage them to keep their information secret by getting them to face each other and hold their books up.
- Give students a minute for A to decide what he/she wants to buy and for B to practise saying the prices.
- Next, A and B roleplay the shop conversation.
- Have whole class feedback where you ask individual students what they bought and how much it cost.

Vocabulary **Adjectives to describe places in a town**
Grammar *There is/are*
Language to go **Talking about places you know**

Interesting places

Language notes

- Students often confuse *it's* and *there's*. *It's* defines something and we use *there's* to say something exists. For example:
  What's that building? **It's** *a museum.*
  There's *a museum in the centre of town.*
- Some students confuse the possessive adjective *their* and *there's*. For example:
  Their *hotel is in the centre of town.*
  There's *a hotel in the centre of town.*
- Students often have problems pronouncing the sound /ð/ and the silent *r* in *there's*. You can help them with the /ð/ sound by highlighting the position of the tongue in front of the front teeth. See the phonemic chart on page 12.
- Learners sometimes have problems with the word order with adjectives and put the adjective after the noun:
  a market busy [*a busy market*].
- In English, adjectives do not change form:
  *a **good** café*
  ***good** cafés.*

Way in

- Ask students about famous places they would recommend visitors see in their country and elicit what you can find in these places. For example: museums, markets, cafés etc. If you think your students are interested, ask them about famous places they know in the UK. Mention Portobello Market to see what the students know about it and if any of them have been there. You may want to mention the film *Notting Hill* with Julia Roberts which shows scenes of the market and the area. If you have the video, you could show a clip.

Vocabulary and speaking

1 Students complete the sentences, then compare their answers, in pairs. Give feedback on the correct answers with the whole class before moving on to Exercise 2.

1 cheap   2 friendly   3 delicious   4 busy

2 Point out the example and do another one with the whole class if necessary. Students work in pairs to finish the activity before whole class feedback.

1 d   2 c   3 e   4 a   5 f   6 b

3 Divide the students into pairs. Do an example with the whole class, using an adjective to ensure that the students use the target language. If you have the video of *Notting Hill*, students can describe the scenes you play of the market.

Reading

4 Students read the website page and decide if the statements are true or false. If students know a lot about Portobello, they could predict the answers before reading.

1 False   2 False   3 False   4 True

Grammar focus

5 Students work in pairs and complete the rules. If students are having problems, highlight the difference between *it's* and *there's*. Focus students' attention on the contractions *there's*; *isn't* and *aren't* and the fact that we don't contract *there are* when writing.

Positive:
We use *there* + **is** + singular nouns.
We use *there* + **are** + plural nouns.
Negative:
We use *there* + **isn't** + singular nouns.
We use *there* + **aren't** + plural nouns.
Questions:
We use **Is** + *there …?* with singular nouns.
We use **Are** + *there …?* with plural nouns.

Practice

6 Point to the picture of the town and do the example with the whole class. Students then work in pairs to complete the activity.
- Do not tell students the correct answers until Exercise 7.

1 There's a small bar.
2 There isn't a market.
3 There aren't any museums.
4 There's a cheap hotel.
5 There are some good cafés.
6 There aren't any interesting shops.

7a Play the recording for the students to check their answers to Exercise 6.

7b Then play the recording again and stop it after the first expression. Ask students to repeat the model as a class. Nominate individual students to repeat and check their pronunciation.
- Repeat this process with the other expressions.

8 Divide students into pairs. Explain that they must find six differences between the pictures without looking at their partner's picture. Demonstrate the activity by taking the role of student A and asking 'Is there a big hotel?' Get student B to answer.

Differences: bar/bookshop; café/hotel; some people/no people; restaurants/supermarket; no cars/cars; market/no market

Get talking …

9 Explain that students must write an entry for the 'Real places' website. Ask students to think of a place they know well either in their town, country or another country.
- Divide the students into pairs to interview each other. Remind them to make notes on their partner's place because they will need these to do the writing activity.

… and writing

10 Students can use the Portobello Market text as a model for their writing. Depending on time, the students can write this in class or for homework, using the notes they made in Exercise 9.
- For an example of a review of a film or place, see **Writing bank** page 148.

LESSON 12

Vocabulary   Everyday activities
Grammar   Adverbs of frequency
Language to go   Talking about how often you do things

The weekend

Language notes

- Students often have problems with adverbial word order. In English, adverbs come after the verb *be* but before all other verbs. For example:
  I am always late.
  I always arrive late.
- Students sometimes have difficulty with the elision in *usually* /juːʒuəli/. Note that there are two ways to pronounce *often*: /ɒfən/ or /ɒftən/.
- Remind students that they make questions with a question word and the auxiliary *do*. For example:
  What do you do in your free time?
  Where do you go after work?

Way in

- Check students know the days of the week. You could write the days on small cards and get students to stand in the correct order from Monday to Sunday.
- Then tell students about your typical weekend (Friday, Saturday, Sunday). Mime or use pictures to convey the meaning of the activities you usually do.

Vocabulary and speaking

1   Students work in pairs to complete the gaps. Give feedback on the correct answers before moving on to Exercise 2.

1 go to church; meet friends; go to the beach
2 go to the gym; stay in; watch a film
3 work late; go for a drink; get a takeaway

2   Divide the students into pairs for this activity. Check that they have matched the texts and photos correctly before going on to talk about the activities. Remind them to use the activities mentioned in Exercise 1.

1 C   2 B   3 A

Listening

3   Explain that students will hear two people describing their free time activities, and so only two of the three pictures will be described.

Speaker 1: A   Speaker 2: C

4   Before you play the recording again, students should read the sentences in Exercise 4 and predict the answers. Then they listen again to complete the activity.

1 works late   2 for a drink   3 cooks   4 to the beach
5 eats

Grammar focus

5a   Point out the example and do another one with the whole class if necessary before asking the students to complete the scale. Write the correct answers on the board.

100%	always
	usually
	often
	sometimes
0%	never

5b   Students then read the example sentences and complete the rules. Highlight the pronunciation problems with *often* and *usually* (see **Language notes**).

The adverb comes *before* the verb.
The adverb comes *after* the verb *be*.

5c   Students complete the question.

How *often* do you stay in?

Practice

6   Students do the activity individually and then check their answers in pairs before feedback.

1 often works; always go   2 are usually
3 often; get; sometimes get   4 never stay;
sometimes watch

7   Do a couple of examples with the whole class about your weekend before asking students to complete the sentences about their weekend.

Get talking

8   Explain that students are going to interview each other about their typical weekends to see how often they do things.
- Divide the students into groups (of four) and demonstrate the activity to check students can ask the questions.
- After the interviews, have whole class feedback where one spokesperson for each group tells the class about the group's results.
- If you have time, students could carry out a class 'frequency survey' on one particular activity and display the results in the form of a bar chart, as in the example below.

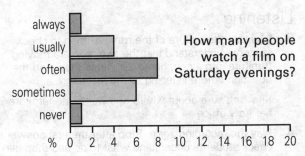

How many people watch a film on Saturday evenings?

Vocabulary Furniture in an office / living room
Grammar Prepositions of place
Language to go Telling someone where things are in a room

Office ... or living room?

Language notes

- The difference between *in front of* and *opposite*, *on* and *above* is not always clear to students. You could use objects in the classroom to highlight the fact that *opposite* is further away than *in front of* and *above* is not touching the object it is connected to.
- Highlight the use of *to* after *next*, for example: *The picture is next to the door.*
- Make sure you highlight the linking in the prepositions, for example:
  in front of, next to.
- Also highlight the weak forms in the prepositions, for example: *opposite* /ˈɒpəzɪt/, *above* /əˈbʌv/.

Way in

- Ask students to name the rooms in a house. Make sure you include *living room* and check they know the meaning of *office*. Avoid covering too many rooms as you don't want the students to get overloaded with vocabulary at this stage.

Vocabulary

1 Point to the picture and do one or two examples with the whole class before students complete the activity in pairs.

> 1 calendar   2 telephone   3 computer   4 desk
> 5 printer   6 sofa   7 chair   8 bin   9 cupboard
> 10 bookcase   11 stereo   12 lamp   13 plant
> 14 armchair

2a Explain the different stress categories by counting out the syllables of the following words on your fingers: *bin, office, living room, front garden.* Highlight the stressed syllables before getting students to complete the table.

2b Model and practise the pronunciation as a class before students practise saying the words to their partner.

> ■ ▪: sofa, bookcase, cupboard, printer, armchair
> ■ ▪ ▪: stereo, telephone, calendar
> ▪ ■ ▪: computer

Listening

3 📼 Use the picture of the removal men to check students understand that the two men are moving furniture into a new home. Students then read the question before listening to the recording.

> She *isn't* sure about where she wants the furniture in her new office.

4 Play the recording again. Stop after the first answer to check students understand what to do and then play the recording to the end.

> desk ✓   computer ✓   printer ✓   telephone ✓   bin ✗
> chair ✗   sofa ✓   calendar ✓   plant ✓   armchair ✓
> cupboard ✓   bookcase ✓   stereo ✓   lamp ✗

Grammar focus

5 Point out the examples before asking students to complete the activity. Depending on your class, this activity could be done individually or as a whole class. If the students have problems, use furniture and objects in the classroom to highlight differences in the meaning.
- Remember to point out the weak forms and linking (see **Language notes**). This would be a good time to drill the students chorally and individually, using the examples from the Grammar focus.

> 4 opposite   5 in front of   6 in   7 on

Practice

6 Students need to use the picture on page 28 to complete this activity. Check the answers with the whole class.

> 1 on   2 under   3 in   4 next to   5 on   6 under
> 7 opposite   8 above

7 Divide the students into pairs and demonstrate this activity with a student to check they know how to do it.
- Encourage the students to use a variety of forms as in the example and not just *Where's the ...?* but *Is there ...?* and *Has she got ...?*

Get talking

8 Demonstrate the activity by drawing a plan of your office or living room on the board without any furniture in it. Ask students to copy your plan, then describe the room to them, while they draw the furniture in the correct position. Then complete your plan on the board so they can check their drawing.
- Tell students to draw a similar plan but of their own office or living room. Students swap plans with their partner. Student A describes the position of the furniture in his / her room while B draws it in the correct place on the plan.
- Make sure students change roles when they have completed the first plan.

Vocabulary   Family
Grammar   Present continuous for now
Language to go   Talking about what your family/friends are doing

Family

Language notes

- English uses the present continuous to express a temporary action happening now or around now and the present simple for a permanent action, true all the time. This often causes problems for students whose language uses one form for both these concepts.
- Students often have problems with the auxiliaries for the present continuous.
  Common mistakes are:
  She's live in Poland. [She lives]
  How often do they watching TV?
  What you doing? instead of *What are you doing?*
  Does he watching TV?
- Students sometimes have problems with the irregular singular and plural forms of *child/children, wife/wives*. Students may also be interested to know the familiar forms of *mother/father* and *grandmother/grandfather*. These vary but the most common are: *mum/dad, granny/grandma, grandad/grampa*.

Way in

- Show students pictures of famous families. Use magazine pictures of royal or celebrity families that the students will recognise. Ask 'Who are they?', 'What are their names?', 'Why are they famous?'. Ideally the pictures should show people doing things, so then students could also use them for practice later in the lesson.
- Alternatively, take in a couple of photos of your family to introduce family vocabulary. Students are usually very interested in finding out more about their teacher.

Vocabulary and speaking

1   Point out the Simpson family tree and ask students to explain how the different characters are related. Point out the example and do one or two with the whole class before students complete the activity in pairs.
- During whole class feedback, check the pronunciation of the words students have problems with.
- Depending on your class, you may want to explain *in-law*. For example: *Selma and Patty are Homer's sisters-in-law* and *Grampa* (Homer's father) *is Marge's father-in-law*.

1 children   2 daughters   3 son   4 father
5 husband   6 sisters   7 brother   8 parents
9 mother   10 aunts   11 uncle   12 grandfather

2   Give students a minute or so to prepare their own family trees before they talk about them in pairs.

Reading

3a   Students predict the answer to Exercise 3a before reading the text. Elicit suggestions from the whole class.
3b   Students then check their answers in pairs, by reading the text.

Bart is happy watching television.

4   Explain that they should predict the answers to Exercise 4 before reading the text for a second time. This prediction gives students a real reason to read as well as providing some support when reading difficult texts.

1 False   2 True   3 False   4 True

Grammar focus

5   Point out the examples before students complete the rules. You can reinforce the meaning by miming actions (*watching, smoking, enjoying*) and asking students to tell you what you are doing. Remind the students that the auxiliary *be* has the same forms as the main verb *be*.

We make the present continuous with
be + verb + *-ing*.

6   Point out the spelling rules, especially that verbs ending in consonant + vowel + consonant form the participle by doubling the last consonant, for example, *get – getting*.

1 talk – talking   2 smoke – smoking   3 get – getting

Practice

7   📖 Use the picture of the Cormack family to revise family vocabulary and teach *older/younger sister*.
- You may want to write some prompts on the board to help students interpret the sounds they hear. Write: *get up, watch TV, talk, play music, eat, play computer games*.
- Play the recording and students write the activity they hear in the present continuous. Check the spelling by writing the correct answers on the board during feedback. Accept contractions and full forms.

1 His wife's eating/having breakfast.
2 His son's watching television/TV.
3 His daughter's listening to music/playing music/ playing the saxophone.
4 Mr Cormack's talking.
5 The children are playing (computer games).

8   Students do this in pairs, then check answers with the whole class.

1 'm/am cooking   2 Are you drinking
3 are you going   4 is she talking   5 're/are playing
6 'm/am watching

Get talking

9   Explain that students need to describe their respective pictures in order to find five differences. Divide students into pairs and demonstrate the activity. Encourage students to use only *yes/no* questions which will force them to use more vocabulary and practise present continuous question forms. When students finish, they should look at their partner's picture to check the five differences.

The father/mother is cooking.
The daughter/son is listening to a personal stereo and dancing.
The son/daughter is watching TV.
The mother/younger daughter is talking on her mobile phone.
The younger daughter/father is working on the computer.

Vocabulary   Food and drink
Function   Making requests
Language to go   Ordering food and drink in a café

In a café

Language notes

- This is the first time students have seen the modal verbs *will* and *can*. They are treated functionally here (so the grammatical complexities regarding auxiliaries and the omission of *to* are not explored at this stage).
- Students often have problems using polite intonation. It is important to highlight that intonation carries meaning and that students with a flat intonation can be seen as rude. The students need to be encouraged to start high.
- Students often have problems with the following sounds:
  I'll /aɪl/
  Can I... /kænaɪ/
- There are a number of words with the long /iː/ sound and the short /ɪ/ sound. Students whose languages do not differentiate between long and short sounds sometimes have problems pronouncing the following words:
  /iː/ *cheese, tea, coffee*
  /ɪ/ *chicken, lettuce*. (See the phonemic chart on page 12.)

Way in

- Brainstorm international words for food on the board. Focusing on international words helps increase the confidence of learners by showing them they know more than they think they know. Common international words include: *pizza, pasta, beer, whisky, sushi, steak, chips (crisps)* and *tea.*

Vocabulary and speaking

1   Explain to students that the picture shows the Liberty Café in New York. Then point to the menu and show the example and where students write in the number from the picture next to the food on the menu. Students complete the activity in pairs.

2 ham   3 cheese   4 chocolate cake   5 apples
6 bananas   7 lemons

2   Students are going to listen to conversations in the café. Play the recording and stop it after the first one to check students know what to do. Then play the recording to the end.
- Students often have problems with intensive listening so play the recording again, this time stopping after each price to give the students time to write it down.

Sandwiches: cheese (with lettuce) – $5.00
Cake: chocolate – $4.85
Hot drinks: small tea – $1.50; large coffee – $1.95
Cold drinks: cola – $1.20
Fruit: apple – $1.25

- Note the way in which US prices are said in the dialogues, for example, *five dollars* ($5), *five-fifty* ($5.50), *five ninety-five* ($5.95) and *fifty cents* ($0.50). Practise saying some prices in US dollars before moving on to Exercise 3.

3   Do this activity yourself with the whole class as an example.
- Give students a minute to choose what they want and then divide them into pairs. Students then tell each other what they have chosen and the total price (not more than $8).

Listening

4   ▭ Play the recording and stop after the first answer to check students know what to do. Then play the recording to the end.
- Play it through once more before checking answers with the whole class.

1 b   2 b   3 a   4 b

Language focus

5   Point out the examples before asking students to complete the rules in the table. Don't go into an explanation of the form at this stage.

I / We *will* have a coffee.
Can I have a tea?

6a   ▭ Play the recording. You may need to do this activity a couple of times. Hold whole class feedback.

6b   ▭ Model the sentences from Exercise 6a. You can do this yourself or use the recording. Ask students to repeat the expressions chorally and then individually.

1 a   2 b

Practice

7   Do the first one as an example with the whole class. Students then finish the activity individually or in pairs. Check the answers with the whole class.

1 I'll; have   2 I; I have; I'll have   3 Can I; I'll

8   Divide the students into pairs. Demonstrate the activity in open class first so you can check for any major pronunciation difficulties.
- Put students into closed pairs to repeat the conversations. Go round the class, monitoring.

Get talking

9   Divide students into two groups, customers and waiters / waitresses.
- Tell the waiters / waitresses to look at page 85 and allocate each one a different menu. Check that they can say *Sorry, we don't have any.*
- Tell the customers to look at the rolecards on page 88 and allocate each rolecard (by number) to different students.
- Set the scene by rearranging the room with the three different cafés in different areas. Customers then go to the different cafés to find out where they can get the food they want (on their rolecard) and how much it costs.
- Have whole class feedback for students to say which café they preferred and why.

Vocabulary Activities at work
Grammar *Can* for ability
Language to go Asking about job skills

Job skills

Language notes

- Students often confuse the use of *can* for requests and *can* for ability. This lesson focuses on *can* for ability. A common mistake for students is using auxiliaries in questions and negatives and the use of *to* as in the following examples:
  I ~~don't can~~ drive. [can't]
  ~~Do you can~~ type? [Can you]
  She can ~~to~~ speak French.
  Can is a modal verb and does not use auxiliaries and is not followed by *to*.
- *Can* causes several pronunciation problems because of the different vowel sounds. (See the phonemic chart on page 12.)
  I can /kən/ drive.
  Can /kaən/ you type?
  Yes, I can /kaən/.
  I can't /kɑːnt/ use a computer.

Way in

- Set the scene by taking in a resumé and several job advertisements, including one for a recruitment consultant's. It would be good to use your own resumé to personalise the activity. Check students understand *resumé* or *CV* (UK English) and explain what information is on it. You may want to invent information, for example, computer qualifications, driving licence or foreign languages.

Vocabulary

1 Point out the example and ask students to work in pairs to complete the activity.

1 read 2 repair 3 sing 4 speak 5 drive 6 type
7 manage

2 Show students the photos in the 'Changing Jobs' article and elicit the two jobs pictured and who does them (Amy is a soldier and tank driver and Gary is a hotel manager). Students then look back at the sentences in Exercise 1 and match each sentence to the correct person.

1 Amy 2 Amy 3 Gary 4 Gary 5 Amy
6 Gary 7 Amy

Reading

3 Ask students where the article comes from and elicit *the Internet*. This will help students become familiar with different text types and encourage them to use the Internet for self-study reading practice.

1 Gary 2 Amy

4 Do the first one as an example with the whole class before they read the text again and complete the activity individually.

1 Gary 2 Amy 3 Gary 4 Gary 5 Amy

Grammar focus

5 You could write the answers to Exercise 4 on the board in order to help students complete the Grammar focus. Highlight the fact that *can* does not use the auxiliary *do* and that there is no *to* before the infinitive.

Positive:
I / You / He / She / We / They *can* drive a car.
Negative:
I / You / He / She / We / They *can't* drive a car.
Questions and short answers:
Can you type?
Yes, I can.
No, I can't.

6a ▭▭ Play the recording and stop it after each expression in order to highlight the weak sound of *can* /kən/ in affirmative statements, the long sound /kɑːnt/ in the negative and the strong sound /kæn/ in short answers.

6b Play the recording again for students to repeat chorally.

7 ▭▭ Play the recording and point out the example. Then play the recording all the way through.
- With weaker classes you may want to stop the recording after each expression and play it more than once.
- This pronunciation practice doubles as intensive listening practice and will help improve the students' overall level of comprehension.

1 can't 2 can 3 Can 4 can't

Practice

8 Make sure students write the full form of the short answers by pointing this out in the example.

1 A: Can you drive a tank?
B: No, I can't.
2 A: Can you type?
B: Yes, I can.
3 A: Can he speak French?
B: Yes, he can.

Get talking

9 Explain that 'Changing Jobs' are a company of career consultants, who advise and help people to find a new career.
- Divide the students into two groups, A and B. Explain that Student A works for the career consultants and is going to use the form to interview Student B to find out which career is best for them. After the interview, make sure students change roles.
- During whole class feedback, students say which career they were advised to do and if they agree with their partner's advice.

LESSON 17

Vocabulary Question words
Grammar Past simple of *be: was, were*
Language to go Talking about childhood memories

Memories

Language notes

- This is the first time in the course that the students are introduced to the past tense. Although the meaning should be clear from the context, students often have problems with word order when making the questions. The negative contractions will also need to be highlighted. Common mistakes include:
  ~~How old your best friend was?~~ [*How old was your best friend?*]
- *Was* and *were* cause several pronunciation problems because of the different weak and strong vowel sounds.
  I was /wəz/ a good student.
  Was /wəz/ he your best friend?
  Yes he was. /wɒz/ No, he wasn't. /wɒzənt/
  Were /wə/ they married?
  Yes, they were. /wɜː/ No, they weren't. /wɜːnt/

Way in

- Brainstorm vocabulary students have studied recently, for example, food and drink, activities at work, family, and write them on the board. Check students know the meaning of the words and then give them one minute to memorise them. After a minute, take the words away. Test the students by saying definitions and asking students to write the corresponding word. This activity will introduce the topic of memory but will also help revise language covered in previous lessons. If your students like competitions, do this as a team activity.

Vocabulary and speaking

1 Focus students on the picture and ask 'Do goldfish have good memories?'. (Goldfish only remember things for a few seconds.) Ask if the students think they have good memories or not. Students then work in pairs to finish the questions with the question words.

> 1 When 2 What 3 How 4 Where 5 How much
> 6 Who

2 Do the first one as an example with the whole class before students complete the activity in open pairs. They can then ask and answer in closed pairs, for further practice. Ask the class who thinks their partner has a good memory.

Listening

3 📼 Explain that students are going to hear two friends playing the board game on page 37. Students read the questions in Exercise 3.
- Play the recording and stop it after the first question to check students know what to do and then play the recording to the end. If you have a strong class, students could listen without looking at the question prompts in Exercise 3. Instead, they listen and tell you which questions they heard.
- Make sure you give feedback on Exercise 3 before moving on to Exercise 4.

> 1 Best holiday ✓ 2 Best friend at school ✗
> 3 First girlfriend ✓ 4 First English lesson ✗

4 Show students that the questions 1 and 3 in Exercise 3 correspond to the answers 1 and 3 in Exercise 4. Then ask the students to remember/guess the questions answered by 2 and 4 in Exercise 4.
- Play the recording again and ask students to check their answers in pairs before giving whole class feedback. You may need to play the recording more than once.

> 1 Greece 2 16 3 Emma 4 14

Grammar focus

5a During whole class feedback, highlight the word order in the questions. You could do this by writing an affirmative sentence and a question on the board and underlining the subject and verb to show the order (for example: *How old were you? I was ten years old.*).

> I/He/She/It *was* fourteen years old.
> I/He/She/It wasn't fourteen years old.
> There *was* a lot to do.
> There *wasn't* a lot to do.
> We/You/They *were* young.
> We/You/They weren't young.
> There *were* beautiful beaches.
> There *weren't* beautiful beaches.

5b Ask students to complete the questions in the past simple tense.

> How old *were* you?
> Where *was* your best holiday?

6 📼 Play the recording and stop it after each expression in order to highlight the individual *was* and *were* sounds. Ask students to repeat the expressions chorally and then individually to check they are pronouncing the sounds correctly. (See the phonemic chart on page 12.)

Practice

7 Do the first one as an example and ask students to work individually to complete the activity. They can compare their answers in pairs, before you check answers with the whole class.

> 1 was; was; Was; wasn't; was 2 were; were; were; were; weren't 3 were; were; were; were

Get talking

8 Divide the students into groups (of three or four). Each student finds a different counter and puts it on *Start*. Explain that to win the game, students need to go from *Start* to *Finish*.
- To move they need to throw a coin. Check students know the meaning of *heads* and *tails* when you toss a coin. Explain that one student starts. If it is *tails*, you move forward two spaces and if it is *heads* you move forward one. When you land on a square, the other students in the group have to use the prompts to ask *was/were* questions and you have to answer.
- Then it is the next student's turn and the process is repeated. It is a good idea to demonstrate the game with one group first, in front of the class, to make sure everyone understands the rules.

LESSON 18

Vocabulary   Everyday activities
Grammar   Past simple regular verbs (positive and negative)
Language to go   Talking about your week

A week in the life of … ?

Language notes

- The students are now familiar with the use of the auxiliary *do* but may have problems using *did/didn't* in questions and negatives in the past.
  Common mistakes include:
  He ~~not called~~ last night. [*didn't call*]
  She ~~no worked~~ at the weekend. [*didn't work*]
- The three different pronunciations of the *-ed* ending for past simple regular verbs is difficult for students as they want to pronounce *-ed* as /ɪd/ every time. Students need to focus on:
  talked /t/   *arrived* /d/   *started* /ɪd/
  Raise the students' awareness of the pronunciation at this stage rather than insist on total accuracy.

Way in

- Write up the following times on the board: *8.00 a.m., 11.00 a.m., 1.30 p.m., 6.00 p.m.* and *11.00 p.m.* Explain that students must ask you *yes/no* questions to find out what you usually do at these times, for example, *Do you have breakfast at eight o'clock?*. This will revise the use of the present simple and question forms as well as leading into the topic of diaries and routines.

Speaking and vocabulary

1   Point out the picture of Martine Andrassi and tell students that she is a theatre manager. Ask what they think is a typical day for her.
- Focus attention on the example in the exercise before asking students to work individually to complete the activity.

> 1 study; want to   2 call   3 start   4 arrive   5 talk
> 6 clean   7 finish

2   Students discuss their routines in pairs. Go round the class, monitoring while they work, and help with any additional vocabulary they need to describe their routines.

Reading

3   Explain that the text is a magazine article in the form of a personal diary. Ask students if they keep diaries before they complete the activity.
- Students read the article to answer Exercise 3.

> 1 True   2 False   3 False   4 True   5 False

Grammar focus

4   You could write the example sentences on the board and do this as a whole class activity.
- The students are given a list of irregular verbs in the Phrasebook. They are not needed in this lesson but you may want to ask your students to look at them before they study Lesson 19.

> 1 We make the past simple positive with infinitive + *-ed*.
> 2 We make the past simple negative with *didn't* + infinitive (without *to*).

5   Point out the different endings of *call*, *arrive* and *study*. Tell students to look at the endings and then complete the table. When you have checked the answers with them ask if they can think of other verbs ending in *-e* or *-y* and write the past tense of those.

> talk – talked; dance – danced; try – tried

6a   Before doing this activity, highlight the difference between voiced and unvoiced sounds. You can do this by asking students to place their thumb and index finger either side of their throat. Alternatively, students can place their hands over their ears.
Model the /s/ sound followed by the /z/ sound (as practised in Lesson 5) and ask the students to repeat these after you. Ask students which sound makes their throat vibrate. Repeat the procedure with /t/ and /d/ sounds.
- Explain that there are pairs of voiced and unvoiced consonants (for example, /s/ /z/ and /t/ /d/). In past simple regular verbs unvoiced *-ed* sounds end in /t/, voiced *-ed* sounds /d/. For verbs ending in *-t* or *-d* the *-ed* ending is pronounced /ɪd/. (See the phonemic chart on page 12).
- Play the first part of the recording, first for students to listen to the pronunciation of *visited*, *called* and *watched*, then again for them to repeat chorally.

6b   Play the recording and stop it after the first one so the students know what to do. Then play the recording to the end. With weaker students, you may need to pause the recording after each word.

> visit*ed*: started; wanted
> call*ed*: studied; arrived; cleaned
> watch*ed*: finished; talked

Practice

7   Make sure students understand that *x* corresponds to a negative sentence, i.e. something that Martine didn't do.

> Thursday: 1 She didn't cook dinner.   2 She called her mother.   3 She didn't watch a movie.
> Friday: 1 She studied Spanish.   2 She started work at 4 p.m.   3 The new concert posters didn't arrive.
> 4 She talked to the musicians.   5 She didn't finish work at 2 a.m.

Get talking

8   Ask students to look at the verbs in the box and decide which ones make them think of something they did last week. Students do this task individually, to give them thinking time.
- Divide the students into groups of four or five. Students tell each other what they did last week.
- Find out how many people did similar activities in whole class feedback.

Vocabulary Common irregular verbs
Grammar Past simple irregular verbs
Language to go Telling a story

Love at first sight

Language notes

- Students often have problems remembering the irregular verbs. This lesson focuses on some of the most common and there is a more extensive list in the Phrasebook. You could do short tests using the list to draw students' attention to the reference list and help them remember the irregular forms.
- Students often confuse *come* and *go*. Use a simple picture on the board to illustrate the difference.

- Students sometimes have problems producing the /ɔ:/ sound in *thought* and *bought*.

Way in

- Draw three faces on the board and label them *Tom, Jane* and *Sue*. Alternatively, use three pictures of different people from a magazine. Draw a heart around the three and ask students to guess what the relationship is between the three people. With weaker classes, you may need to support the students by asking questions, for example, 'Does Jane love Tom? Does Tom love Jane? Why?' Spend a couple of minutes predicting different possible stories before moving on to the story in the lesson.

Vocabulary and speaking

1 Point out the example and do another one with the whole class if necessary. Explain that some verbs can go with more than one picture.

> meet someone – E, F; go to her house – G; give presents – A; leave her house – B; fall in love – F, H; buy her flowers – C; say 'no' – D; see him with her – H

2 Students should identify the first picture in the story (E) as a whole class, before finishing the activity in groups of three. At this stage they can use the infinitives in the word box, not the past tense. Do not check the answers with students yet.

> Correct order: 1 E 2 G 3 C 4 A 5 D 6 B 7 F 8 H

Listening

3 ▭▭ Play the recording for the students to check they have the correct order. You may need to play the recording more than once.
- During feedback for ranking activities, it can be useful to focus on the differences in students' answers. Write the number of the pictures the students disagree about on the board and play the section of the recording that gives the right answer again.
- This guided intensive listening practice can help with comprehension as well as boost students' confidence.

Grammar focus

4a This activity is designed to encourage students to notice the language in context. However, do not get sidetracked by students asking too many questions about vocabulary that is not the main aim of the lesson.
- When giving whole class feedback, help students with the pronunciation of the words they have difficulties with. You can do this by modelling the words and asking the students to repeat them chorally and then individually.

> meet – met; fall – fell; go – went; buy – bought; come – came; give – gave; say – said; leave – left; see – saw

4b Focus attention on the rule, then ask students to complete the example in pairs.

> Example: He *didn't see* her.
> (not He didn't saw her.)

Practice

5 Create interest in the story by asking questions about the picture before students complete the sentences. For example: *Where's Violet? Why is she there? What's Giovanni's job? How do they feel about each other?* Then do the first one as an example with the whole class.

> 1 met 2 fell 3 was 4 gave 5 said 6 came
> 7 thought 8 left 9 went 10 saw 11 didn't love

Get talking …

6 Point to the three characters in the story and elicit their names. Explain that students must work in pairs to retell the story so far, and continue it by imagining what happened next to Jane. Start by giving an example before letting the students continue.
For example: *Jane met Tom at a party. The next day he came to her house …*
- After telling the story once, you could also regroup the students and get them to tell their story to their new partner.

… and writing

7 The follow up writing activity can be done in class or at home. Show students the beginning of the letter and ask them to finish the sentence to check they know what to do. This would be a good opportunity to go over the layout of an informal personal letter.
- For an example of an informal letter and a story, see **Writing bank** pages 147 and 149.

Vocabulary Verbs and nouns: important events in life
Grammar Past simple (questions)
Language to go Asking questions to find out about people's lives

Life and times

Language notes

- Although students are familiar with question forms with auxiliaries in the present simple, the use of *did* still causes problems. Students often omit it or use it with the verb *be*.
  Common mistakes include:
  When ~~you leave~~ school? [*did you leave?*]
  When ~~did you went~~ to the USA? [*did you go*]
  When ~~did~~ you born? [*were*]
- Students sometimes have problems producing the *Did you ...?* /dɪdʒə/ sound in connected speech.

Way in

- Play 'Twenty Questions' to introduce the topic of famous people and revise the use of question forms. Brainstorm the names of national/international celebrities. Choose a famous person and explain that students must ask you a maximum of twenty 'yes/no' questions to identify who the famous person is (for example: *Is this person a man? Is he an actor? Is he Australian?*).
- Once students have guessed who the famous person is, you could move into the vocabulary or get the students to play the game again in groups or pairs.

Vocabulary and speaking

1 Focus the students' attention on the photo and ask the question to the whole class.

> The actress in the photo is Julia Roberts.

- Students then work in pairs to discuss what they know about her.

2 Point out the example and do another one with the class if necessary before students complete the activity in pairs.

> 1 get   2 go   3 start/finish   4 move   5 become
> 6 have   7 make   8 do

Reading

3 Students guess the answers to the matching activity before they read the text to check their answers.

> 1967 – she was born
> 1984 – she moved to New York
> 1986 – she made her first film
> 1993 – she got married
> 1995 – she got divorced

Grammar focus

4 Check students know the short answer form for the 'yes/no' question (*Yes, she did./No, she didn't.*). It is a good idea to elicit other types of question words that you can use as well as the example *when* (for example, *where, what, who, why*).

> *Did* she want to work with animals?
> When *did* she make her first film?

Practice

5 Students work in pairs to complete the activity. Wait until Exercise 6 to check the answers.

> 1 did she work?   2 Did she go to university?
> 3 did she move to New York?   4 Did she get married?
> 5 did she get divorced?

6a 📼 Students listen to the recording and check their answers to Exercise 5. Stop the recording after each question so that students are clear on the word order. You could write the questions on the board to ensure that the students have a correct written record.

6b Play the recording again for students to listen and repeat the questions.

7 Divide the students into pairs and explain that each student has different questions and information about Kate Winslet.
- Students use their prompts to write questions, which they ask their partner. They also have information about Kate Winslet, which they must use to answer their partner's questions.
- Encourage students to keep their information secret by moving their seats and keeping their book raised. This can help increase motivation as students really need to communicate to carry out the activity.
- Students look at their partner's book to check they have the correct information.

Get talking ...

8 Explain that students are going to interview their partner in order to write an article all about them in a similar style to the Julia Roberts article.
- Give students five minutes to prepare interesting questions to use in the interview. You could elicit a few examples to help the students come up with ideas and make their questions more interesting.
- Remind students to take notes on their partner's answers so they can complete the writing follow up in Exercise 9.

... and writing

9 Depending on time, you can do this writing follow up in class or at home. Encourage the students to use the text about Julia Roberts as a model, writing the interview questions and their partner's answers to these.

Vocabulary Numbers
Grammar Questions with *How* + adjective
Language to go Asking for and giving measurements

Quiz show

Language notes

- Students often have problems with word order in the questions with *How* + adjective:
  ~~How fast a cheetah is?~~ [*How fast is a cheetah?*]
- Students often have problems with the use of *and* in numbers including *hundred* and *thousand*. For example, ~~two hundred thirty-five~~ [*two hundred and thirty-five*] *two thousand ~~and~~ three hundred*
- Students sometimes insert a plural *s* after *hundred* and *thousand*. For example:
  five ~~hundreds~~ [*five hundred*]
  three ~~thousands~~ [*three thousand*]
- Unlike some other languages, English uses a decimal point in numbers like 7.5 (*seven point five*) and a comma in numbers like 7,500 (*seven thousand, five hundred*).

Way in

- Brainstorm the names of famous TV quiz shows and their cash prizes. Ask students to tell you what happens in each show.
- Ask if students like quiz shows, which are their favourites and why.

Vocabulary and speaking

1 Do the first one as an example with the whole class. After students finish, get them to read the note on punctuation used in numbers. Alternatively, highlight this on the board.

1 – 15	2 – 25	3 – 50	4 – 100	5 – 205	6 – 235
7 – 1,050	8 – 1,200	9 – 75,000	10 – 105,000		

2 🎧 Play the recording for students to check their answers to Exercise 1. Check that students have used the correct punctuation by writing the answers on the board.
- Note that the weak pronunciation of *and* which is used to link two numbers is difficult for some students to pronounce: *Three hundred and /ən/ fifty.*
- Model a couple of the numbers for the students to repeat chorally and then individually. Then students practise saying the numbers in pairs.
- Practise more numbers by writing numbers at random on the board and asking students how to say them, or dictating numbers and asking students to write them down in figures.

3 🎧 Explain that students are going to listen to a TV quiz show. Play the recording but pause after the first answer to check students know what to do. Then play the recording to the end.
- You may need to play it a couple of times before giving whole class feedback.

1 £25	2 £50	6 £1,050	8 £ 3,750	11 £25,500	
14 £ 500,000					

4 Demonstrate the activity before students complete the activity in pairs.

Listening

5 Students read and answer the quiz show questions, discussing them in pairs.

6 🎧 Play the recording for the students to check their answers to Exercise 5.

12 A	13 B	14 A

Grammar focus

7 Point out the examples and the illustrations before eliciting the answers from the whole class. If your students are interested, they could guess the answers to the questions.

1 far	2 heavy	3 deep

Extra information: Cape Town is 7,189 km from Cairo. An African elephant weighs 4,000–6,000 kg. Lake Baikal is the deepest lake in the world at 1,637 m (at its deepest point).

Practice

8 Students work in pairs to complete the activity. Give whole class feedback on the question forms before the students find out the answers in Exercise 9.

Canada
1 How deep is Hudson Bay?
2 How high is the CN Tower in Toronto?
3 How fast is a grizzly bear?
4 How far is Vancouver from Montreal?
5 How long is the Mackenzie River?

Australia
1 How high is Uluru (Ayers Rock)?
2 How fast are kangaroos?
3 How long is the Murray River?
4 How far is Sydney from Darwin?
5 How heavy are koala bears?

9 Divide the students into pairs, A and B. Students then ask and answer the questions about Canada and Australia using the information at the back of the book.

Get writing ...

10 Divide the students into two groups, A and B. You could encourage the students to imagine they are on a general knowledge quiz show by getting them to invent a name for the show.
- Explain that each group has three quiz questions, with the correct answer given to each. They must invent and write down three false answers, to make a total of four answers for each question.

... and talking

11 Students regroup into pairs of A and B and test their new partner. If your class likes competitions, ask the students to keep a score on which team got the most answers right, A or B.

Vocabulary Countable and uncountable nouns
Grammar Expressions of quantity
Language to go Talking about food you like

Sweet and savoury

Language notes

- Although the concept of countable and uncountable nouns exists in different languages, students often have problems because not all uncountable words in English are uncountable in their language. Students sometimes add -s to uncountable nouns, for example:
  Can I have some butters? [butter]
- Some words can be both countable and uncountable depending on their meaning. Countable nouns refer to something in particular while uncountable nouns express a general concept:
  I like coffee. (general concept – uncountable)
  I'd like a coffee. (particular instance – countable)
- At this level, it is easiest to tell students that we use many and much in negatives and questions and a lot of with affirmative sentences.
- Students often have problems with a lot (of) in the short answer by adding of when there is no noun following. For example:
  How much chocolate do you eat?
  A lot of.

Way in

- Revise the food and drink vocabulary from Lesson 15. Tell students to imagine they are hungry and they can go into a café and buy whatever food and drink they want. In pairs, they tell their partner what they want to eat.

Vocabulary and speaking

1 Describe shopping basket 1 as an example with the whole class. In feedback, point to the individual items in the pictures and elicit the correct word for each.
   - This would be a good opportunity to quickly go over the pronunciation of the food vocabulary the students often have problems with (such as chocolate /tʃɒklət/ and biscuits /bɪskɪts/).

2 Check that the students know the meaning of sweet and savoury by eliciting two more examples in the categories. Then divide the students into pairs to complete the activity.
   - Some items may provoke discussion, especially biscuits and wine, as biscuits can be savoury (for example, cheese biscuits) and wine can be sweet. Accept both categories, but ask students to justify their choice with examples.

Suggestions
Sweet: chocolate; biscuits; ice cream; cakes; sweets; cola; (wine)
Savoury: cheese; crisps; wine; bread; butter; coffee; tomato ketchup; (biscuits)

Listening

3 Students predict which shopping basket belongs to which shopper in the photos. Although this is guesswork, it personalises the activity and gives students a real reason to listen.

4 ▭ Play the recording and ask the students to check their predictions and match the people to the shopping baskets.

1 Melanie   2 Tim   3 Lorraine

Grammar focus

5 Highlight the rules. You could do this by using gestures to show what you can and can't count. Do one or two examples with the whole class before students complete the table.

Countable: biscuits; crisps; cakes; sweets
Uncountable: chocolate; ice cream; wine; bread; butter; coffee; cheese; tomato ketchup; cola

   - Depending on your class, you may want to highlight ways of counting uncountable foods. For example:
     a cup of coffee, two coffees, a packet of butter, a bar of chocolate, a bottle of wine, a can of cola, a bottle of ketchup, a loaf of bread.

6 After students have used the table to complete the rules, highlight the short answers of not much / many and a lot.
   - This would be a good time to focus on the pronunciation of a lot of /əlɒtəv/ in connected speech, by modelling and drilling the example sentences.

1 We use many with countable nouns in questions and negatives.
2 We use much with uncountable nouns in questions and negatives.
3 We use a lot of with countable and uncountable nouns in positive sentences.

Practice

7 Point out the example and ask students to complete the activity in pairs.

1 many; many   2 much; a lot of   3 much; much; a lot of   4 many; a lot   5 much; A lot   6 much; much

Get talking

8 Explain that students are going to interview their partner to see if they are a sweet or savoury person. Get students to add more items to the sweet and savoury columns of the questionnaire individually.
   - Check they can make correct questions by pointing out the example, and practising similar exchanges in open pairs. When students have finished interviewing each other, have whole class feedback to see how many students were 'sweet' and how many were 'savoury'.

LESSON 23

Vocabulary Verbs and nouns describing changes in life
Grammar *Going to* for future plans
Language to go Talking about future plans

Big plans

Language notes

- Students often overuse *will* instead of *going to* when describing future plans which have already been made before the moment of speaking.
- With the verbs *come* and *go*, we often do not use the full *going to* future form, but use the present continuous for the future instead. The students are familiar with the form of the present continuous but not with its meaning of future arrangements. For example, we normally say *We're going on holiday.* instead of *We're going to go on holiday.*
- The pronunciation of *going to* can cause problems. In connected speech, *going to* sounds like /gəʊɪŋ tə/.

Way in

- Elicit the date and the year from the students and write it on the board. Then write up the same date but one year in the future / past. Next, tell the students about big changes you made in the past and want to make in the future. For example, *Last year I got married. Next year I want to study Chinese.*

Vocabulary and speaking

1 Focus students' attention on the pictures of Simon and Emily Wilkinson and their house in the country. Ask where they are and elicit: the city, the country. Do the first one as an example with the whole class, before students complete the activity.

> 1 earn 2 change 3 build 4 retire

2 Students work individually to complete Exercise 2 then check their answers in pairs before whole class feedback.

> 1 d 2 e 3 b 4 c 5 a

3 Tell the class a couple of things you want to do in the future from the vocabulary in Exercises 1 and 2 (for example, *I want to go to China.*). Then give students a minute to think of their choices before they discuss their answers in pairs.

Reading

4 Make sure students realise the article is about the people in Exercise 1. Encourage students to read the questions before they start reading the text. After reading the article, ask the students to discuss their answers in pairs before holding whole class feedback.

> 1 The city. 2 No. 3 The country. 4 Yes.

5 Point out the examples in the table and do one more so the students know exactly what they are doing.

> City: successful job, lots of money, beautiful flat, computer consultants
> Country: no electricity; no shower; no supermarket; build a house; grow vegetables; offer holidays

Grammar focus

6a When the students have completed the rule, you may want to highlight the use of the verb *be* as an auxiliary and remind students of the rules about contractions, especially in short answers (*Yes, I am./No, I'm not.*).

> We use *am/is/are* + *going to* + infinitive to talk about future plans.

6b Students complete the question forms in pairs.

> 1 What *are* they *going to* do?
> 2 A: *Are* you *going to* build a house?
>   B: Yes, we are./No, we aren't.

7 📖 Play the recording for students to repeat the expressions chorally and individually. Expressions with *going to* are quite long so backchaining the sentences can really help students.

Practice

8 Students complete the activity in pairs, writing out the whole sentences.
- Encourage contracted forms, but accept full forms as correct.

> 1 What are they going to do next year?
> 2 Emily's/Emily is going to lose weight.
> 3 Simon's/Simon is going to give up smoking.
> 4 They aren't/are not going to earn much money.
> 5 They're/They are going to retire to the countryside.
> 6 Are they going (to go) abroad?
> 7 They aren't/are not going to leave the Cumberland Mountains.
> 8 Emily's/Emily is going to learn to cook meals for a lot of people.

Get talking

9 Explain that students must look at the lists of plans in the notes and tick any which they, personally, are planning for the future.
- Each student should add two more plans (which are true for them) to each list.
- In pairs, they interview their partner about their future plans to see if they are going to make any big changes. When students have finished, have a short class discussion about who is going to change their lives the most.

LESSON 24

Vocabulary Parts of a public building; American English
Grammar Prepositions of movement
Language to go Asking and giving directions

It's on the right

Language notes

- Directions often cause students problems because of the number of exponents they have to remember. This lesson focuses on directions within a building but many of the expressions can be used to give directions in other situations. Common mistakes include:
  Turn ~~on the~~ right.
  It's ~~at~~ the right. [on]
- Students sometimes confuse *go down to the first floor* and *go down the corridor*. To avoid this confusion, this lesson introduces *go along the corridor* instead of *go down the corridor.*
- The difference between *first floor* and *ground floor* in US and UK English sometimes causes confusion. Point this out when you reach Exercise 2.

Way in

- Set the scene and prepare students for some of the practice activities by revising the names of different rooms. Draw a plan of the school / your house. Describe what people do in each room and elicit the name of the room.
  For example: *You can cook in this room.* (*Kitchen*).
- If you draw a plan of the school, this may help pre-teach some of the vocabulary in Exercise 1.

Vocabulary

1 Students do this activity in pairs, labelling the different places in the hotel plan.

> 1 first floor   2 ground floor   3 lift   4 gift shop
> 5 corridor   6 stairs   7 toilets   8 basement
> 9 car park

2a Point out the picture and the differences in describing floors in British and American English. *First floor* has a different meaning in British and American English.

2b Students complete the exercise then check answers with the whole class. Point out the different spellings of *theatre / theater* in British and American English.

> 1 b   2 d   3 e   4 a   5 c

- If students are interested in learning more about the difference between British and American English, give them some other examples. Write the British words on the left of the board and the American equivalents, jumbled, on the right. Ask students to work in pairs to match the words.
- Some common words to use for this, which occur in the coursebook are:

British English	American English
biscuits	cookies
holiday	vacation
trousers	pants
postcode	zipcode
crisps	potato chips
cupboard	closet
autumn	fall

Listening

3 Students read the questions before listening to the recording all the way through. Check the students' answers and play the recording again if students are having problems.

> 1 Red Lounge   2 lift   3 second floor

Grammar focus

4 When students have completed the activity, you may want to highlight the pronunciation of the different expressions. Pick a couple of exponents and focus on the linking. For example:
It's‿on the left.
Come out‿of the lift.

> 1 A   2 D   3 B   4 F   5 C   6 E

Practice

5 Explain that the dialogues correspond to the hotel plan. Do the first one as an example with the whole class and then get the students to finish the exercise in pairs. Do not give feedback on the answers at this stage.

6 Play the recording for students to listen and check their answers to Exercise 5. Pause after each gap to make sure that the students have got the correct answers.
- If your students are still having problems with pronunciation, use the model on the tape to get students repeating the directions chorally and individually.

> 1 up; out of; right; along; left
> 2 left; past; right; right
> 3 past; down; out of; in front of

Get talking

7 Divide students into pairs, Student A and Student B. Explain that each pair needs to give directions in order to complete their hotel plans.
- Encourage students to get into character by standing up and getting one student to be the receptionist and one the hotel guest before they practise the directions.

8 Demonstrate the activity by asking how to get from the classroom to reception.
- Get students to think of two places in the building. Students then practise their new conversations in pairs.
- If your building is very small, you can extend the activity to include the nearby streets. By personalising the situation, you can make the language more relevant and hopefully more memorable.

LESSON 25

Vocabulary Weather
Grammar Linking words: *because, so, but, although*
Language to go Describing climate and lifestyle

Hot and sunny

Language notes

- Avoid using the adjectives *rainy* and *snowy* and instead concentrate on the verbs *it's raining/snowing*. *Rainy* and *snowy* are usually only used with a noun (for example, *a rainy day*).
- Students often have problems understanding the difference between reason and result expressed by *because* and *so*. Make sure you have thought of other clear examples to use to back up the ones in the Grammar focus.

Way in

- Introduce the theme of the lesson by asking students to think of their perfect place to take a city break at the coming weekend. This could be in their area, country or worldwide. You could give an example yourself before putting the students into pairs to talk about what place they have chosen and why.

Vocabulary and speaking

1   Students describe the pictures in pairs. During feedback, go over all four pictures with the whole class and check that the students are using the appropriate vocabulary.

2   Do this as a whole class activity. You may need to check the pronunciation of the seasons, especially *autumn* before you ask a number of individual students the questions about seasons.

> Picture 1: summer   Picture 2: winter
> Picture 3: spring   Picture 4: autumn (fall)

Reading

3   Point to the title of the article and predict what activities you could do on a weekend break in Boston in summer and winter. Students complete the reading activity. They can write the six activities, or underline the activities in the text.
   - Point out to students that we write *25–30°C*, but we say *25 to 30 degrees Celsius* or *Centigrade*.

> Summer: go to the beach; the lakes, outdoor concerts; live jazz festivals; 4 July celebrations
> Winter: go skiing and snowboarding; watch football on TV; sit in front of the fire; eat New England Clam Chowder

4   Students discuss the questions in pairs.

Grammar focus

5a Use the examples to highlight the meaning and form of the linking words. (*Although* and *but* have the same meaning and *because* and *so* mean the same.) Highlight the different possible word order combinations of *because* and the punctuation with *so*.

5b Students read the article again and find more examples. This type of activity encourages the students to observe language in context in the material they read both in and out of the classroom.
   - Giving feedback on this type of activity is sometimes slow and confusing with students having to read out sentences. If possible, copy the key and give it to the students on an OHP or a photocopy.

> *Although* it is very hot in Boston in the summer, the city is usually very quiet *because* many Bostonians go to the beaches in Cape Cod or the lakes of Maine. Summer is also the time for festivals in the countryside *so* don't miss the outdoor concerts, live jazz festivals and the 4 July celebrations. Wear T-shirts and shorts *because* it's usually 20–35°C.
> Winter is very cold in Boston *but* it is only three months of the year. It snows in December and January *so* you can go skiing and snowboarding. In the evening you can watch American football on TV, sit in front of the fire and eat New England Clam Chowder, a delicious fish soup.

Practice

6   Students complete the activity in pairs, then check their answers in whole class feedback.

> 1 so   2 because   3 but; because   4 Although
> 5 because   6 Although; so   7 so

7   Point out the example and do one or two more with the whole class if necessary. Focus on the pronunciation of *because* /bɪkɒs/ and *although* /ɔːlðəʊ/ as their spelling can confuse students.
   - Students use the weather vocabulary to complete this activity individually before regrouping to tell their partner about their personal preferences.

Get talking ...

8   Explain that students need to plan and then present an advice sheet about the climate and lifestyle in their area. Divide students into groups (of four) and give them a few minutes to make notes and decide how to present the information as a group. Then get the groups to present their advice to the whole class.
   - Make sure that the students do not just read their notes and encourage the listeners to ask questions about the information they hear.
   - You could vary the activity by getting the students to talk about different areas/places and by giving specific information about the visitors (for example, twenty students aged 18–24 or two families with children. This will alter the type of advice given.
   - In a multilingual class it would be appropriate to divide the students into nationality groups for this activity.

... and writing

9   Depending on time, this could be done in class or as homework. It should be based on the notes students made in Exercise 8.
   - For an example of an e-mail, see **Writing bank** page 150.

Vocabulary Dates
Grammar Time prepositions: *in, on, at*
Language to go Talking about memorable times

A new year

Language notes

- Prepositions of time often cause a lot of confusion because of L1 interference so students need to be encouraged to find ways of remembering them.
- US and UK dates are often confusing because of their different written format. For example, a date like 3/2/02 could be *3 February* (UK) or *2 March* (US). In US English, dates consist of *month/day/year* whereas in UK English dates are *day/month/year*.
- When saying dates, students often omit the article *the* and the preposition *of*. Common mistakes include: *the* ~~thirty-one~~ *December* [*thirty-first of*]

Way in

- Write up one or two important dates in your life. Explain that students must ask you 'yes / no' questions to find out why it is an important date for you. Make sure students know enough vocabulary to ask questions about your date and if they are having problems, give them hints.
- Important events could include meeting a famous person, a once-in-a-lifetime experience you have had, a special holiday, birth of a child, etc.

Vocabulary and speaking

1 Discuss the questions with the whole class and establish that the pictures show the eclipse of the sun, the millennium bug symbol and the millennium celebrations in Sydney.

> **Extra information:** The millennium bug was the symbol used in a government campaign in the UK, aimed at making people aware that there could be a problem with some computers when the date changed from 31/12/99 to 1/1/00.

2a You may like to do this activity on the board with the whole class. Highlight the different ways of saying the dates, concentrating on the use of *the* and *of*. Also show the different ways of saying and writing the dates in US and UK English.

2b Before students do this activity, make sure they are familiar with the names of months.
- Give examples of two different ways of expressing the year: 1/7/01 = *The first of July* **oh-one**. or *The first of July* **two thousand and one**.
- Students practise saying the dates in pairs. Alternatively, you could ask one student to say a date and the other to write it.

> **Extra information:** At present, the years 2001 and 2002 are pronounced *two thousand and one, two thousand and two*. In the future, this could change to the previous system where the year was pronounced in two stages. For example, 2010 would be pronounced *twenty ten*.

3 Students listen to the recording to check their answers. Play the recording again and pause after each date. Students repeat the dates chorally and individually.

Listening

4 Focus students' attention on the pictures about 1999 before playing the recording all the way through for students to match the speakers to the pictures.

> Dave: 2   Jennifer: 1   George: 3

5 Play the recording again for the students to complete Exercise 5.

> 1 b   2 c   3 a

Grammar focus

6 After students complete the table, highlight the fact that time expressions usually come at the end of a sentence but can also come at the beginning, especially to show emphasis or contrast. For example:
What are you doing at the weekend?
On Saturday, I'm playing tennis but I don't know about Sunday.
- You could also mention the difference between *on the weekend* in US English and *at the weekend* in UK English.

> *In:* November; 1999; the evening
> *On:* 11th August; Monday; Christmas Day
> *At:* ten o'clock; the weekend; Christmas / Easter; lunch

Practice

7 Point out the example and then ask students to finish the activity in pairs.

> 1 at; on   2 on   3 in   4 on   5 on   6 in   7 in   8 at

Get talking

8 Give students a few minutes to think of five important dates in their life and go round and help with any vocabulary the students ask for. You may need to prompt students to help them think of important dates by suggesting birthdays, public holidays, special festivals or the beginning or end of term. Remind them of the types of dates you chose in the Way in section.
- Students then talk in pairs about their dates. Encourage students to ask follow up questions but make sure that students do not simply read out their notes. Ask them to put their notes away and only refer to them quickly if they really have to.
- Students can change partners and talk about their special events to another partner.

Vocabulary Everyday requests
Function Permission and requests
Language to go Asking for things and giving a response

Requests

Language notes

- Students often have difficulties with the form of *could*. There is no auxiliary and no *to* between *could* and the infinitive. Common mistakes include:
  Could I ~~to~~ borrow your pencil?
  ~~Do I could~~ help you? [*Could I*]
- *Could* is the past form of *can* but students need to know that the concept is present. If you think it will help your students, tell them that *Can I …?* and *Could I …?* mean the same but *Could I …?* is more polite.
- When refusing requests, it is common to apologise and then give a reason. For example:
  A: *Could I borrow your dictionary?*
  B: *Sorry, but I'm using it.*
- A flat intonation is likely to be interpreted as rudeness on the part of the listener who might then reject the request. Encourage students to exaggerate their intonation and use a high voice range.

Way in

- Ask students 'Could I collect the homework? Could I borrow a pen? Could you open the window?' to introduce the theme of making requests. You could lead into Exercise 1 by making a couple of rude requests. For example, 'Give me your pen'. This will highlight the contrast and make it easier to check the meaning of *polite*.

Reading and speaking

1 Check students know the meaning of *polite* before they discuss Exercise 1 in pairs. Tell students not to read the quiz yet.

2 Students can do the quiz individually. They then work in pairs to ask and answer the questions in the quiz orally. In pairs, they compare their answers and add their scores up. Go round the class and find out who is the most polite.

Vocabulary

3 Point out the example and do another one with the whole class if necessary. Tell students that if they need help they should look at the quiz again, and see how these verbs are used.

1 call	2 pass	3 recommend	4 say	5 pay
6 borrow	7 accept			

Language focus

4 Students read the examples from the quiz to help them complete the rules for *could* with requests.

1 We use **Could** + **I** + infinitive (without *to*) to ask for things.
2 We use **Could** + **you** + infinitive (without *to*) to ask other people to do things.
3 To say '*Yes*' we use *Yes, sure.* or **Yes, of course**.
4 To say '*No*' we use *Sorry, and* **I'm afraid** and give a reason.

5 Play the recording and pause it after each *request*. The expressions are long and could be difficult for the students, so be ready to break them down into smaller parts and backchain. This involves drilling the last words first.
- Make sure you encourage the students to exaggerate their intonation by using gestures to show how the intonation rises and falls.

Practice

6 Point out the example and do another one with the whole class if necessary. Students then do this activity in pairs.
- Do not give feedback at this stage but make a note of any problems that you hear while monitoring the students.

1 Could you pass the wine, please?
2 Could I borrow your car, please?
3 Could I pay by credit card?
4 Could you say that again, please?
5 Could you recommend a good restaurant?
6 Could I use your mobile phone?
7 Could I have a coffee, please?
8 Could you tell me the way to the Tower Hotel?

7 Again students complete this in pairs but do not give feedback at this stage, as they check their answers in Exercise 8.

8 Students listen to the recording to check their answers to Exercises 6 and 7.
- Explain that *please* is optional in the answers. Some of the requests on the recording include *please* and others do not.
- If you have time, this would be a good opportunity to practise saying the expressions after the tape. Focus on the ones that cause the most problems for the students.

1 a	2 e	3 d	4 b	5 c	6 f	7 h	8 g

Get talking …

9 Divide the students into pairs and explain that each student is going to ask or accept/refuse requests using their prompts. Give students a few minutes to prepare their requests and remind them that they can only accept requests three times. This should encourage them to listen carefully to the requests in order to decide if they should accept or refuse them.

… and writing

10 Students write a note with a short request on. Ask them to pass the note to another student, who must write an answer, accepting or refusing the request, and pass it back.
- For an example of short notes and replies see **Writing bank** page 151.

LESSON 28

Vocabulary Adjectives to describe places
Grammar Comparatives
Language to go Comparing places in your country

North and south

Language notes

- Although the concept is clear, students sometimes have problems with the form of comparatives. Students need help with spelling and the use of *more*. Common mistakes include:
  The north is ~~more~~ hotter than the south.
  The north is hotter ~~that~~ the south. [than]
- Students often sound unnatural because they stress each word equally and slowly. Highlight the weak pronunciation of *than* /ðən/ and emphasise the main stress in the sentence to help students sound more natural. For example:
  The <u>north</u> is <u>hotter</u> than the <u>south</u>.

Way in

- Draw a compass on the board and elicit the compass points: *north*, *south*, *east* and *west*. Ask students to think about the north and south of their country and brainstorm adjectives that describe it. If teaching a multicultural class, you can get them to discuss the host country.

Vocabulary and speaking

1 Focus students' attention on the photos of New Zealand and get them to discuss the questions in Exercise 1 in pairs. The topic of north and south can create a lot of discussion so if students are interested, have whole class feedback to listen to the opinions of the class.
   - As with any potentially controversial topic, make sure you're ready to change the direction of the discussion if someone suggests something that could be seen as offensive by other students.

2 Point out the example and students then do this exercise in pairs. During whole class feedback, check that students know the meaning of all the adjectives. You could do this by getting students to give you a sentence containing the adjective with an appropriate adjective + noun combination.

   1 delicious   2 dirty   3 modern   4 small

3 Students talk in pairs about the pictures of New Zealand, using the vocabulary from Exercise 2.

Listening

4 Focus students' attention on the map of New Zealand and quickly pronounce the names of the towns so the students will be able to recognise them.
   Auckland /ɔːklənd/;
   Rotorua /rəʊtəruːə/;
   Marlborough /mɑːlbərə/;
   Queenstown /kwiːnstaʊn/.
   - Play the recording all the way to the end.

   Speaker 1: North   Speaker 2: South
   Speaker 3: South

5 Give students time to read through the descriptions of places before playing the recording again so students can complete the matching activity.

   1 c   2 a   3 b

Grammar focus

6 After students have completed the table, highlight the spelling rules (especially the doubling of letters) and the irregular comparative adjectives.

	Adjective	Comparative
1 syllable	clean nice	cleaner than nicer than
Ends with 1 consonant + 1 vowel + 1 consonant	big flat wet	*bigger than* flatter than *wetter than*
Ends with 'y'	friendly dry dirty	friendlier than *drier than* dirtier than
2 syllables or more	cosmopolitan modern exciting mountainous	more cosmopolitan than *more modern than* *more exciting than* more mountainous than
Irregular	good bad	better than worse than

7 Play the recording and pause it after each item. The expressions can be difficult for students, so be ready to break them down into smaller parts and backchain. Students then repeat the expressions chorally and individually to check their pronunciation. Make sure you focus on the weak sound in than /ðən/ and emphasise the stressed adjective.

Practice

8 Point out the example and do another one with the whole class if necessary. Students then do this activity in pairs.

   1 Chicago is more expensive than New Orleans.
   2 New York is more cosmopolitan than Dallas.
   3 The south of France is drier than the north.
   4 The north of Italy is wetter than the south.
   5 The south of Poland is more mountainous than the north.
   6 Brasilia is more modern than Rio.
   7 The north of Russia is colder than the south.
   8 Holland is flatter than Germany.

Get talking

9 Write *City/Region of the Year* on the board and explain that students are going to discuss different places in order to decide which place should win this competition. Check students know the meaning of *region*. Divide the class into groups (of four) to choose their top two places in their country. Encourage students to think about why one place is better than the other using the categories provided to help them.
   - For feedback, get each group to present their choices to the whole class and encourage a class discussion.
   - If you are teaching a multilingual class, students should choose a place in the host country/the world or work in nationality groups.
   - If appropriate, students can discuss the differences between the north and south of their country and decide which is the best region.

Vocabulary	Adjectives to describe restaurants
Grammar	Superlatives
Language to go	Describing restaurants

The best food in town

Language notes

- As with comparatives the concept is clear, but students have problems with the form of superlatives. Students need help with spelling and the use of the definite article (*the* with *most*). Common mistakes include:
  McDonald's is the ~~most cheap~~. [*cheapest*]
  McDonald's is ~~cheapest~~. [*the cheapest*]
- The complexity of the form also makes the expressions difficult to pronounce. Students often sound stilted because they stress each word equally and slowly.

Way in

- Talk about your favourite restaurant and why you like it. Then students describe their favourite restaurant in pairs. If students do not have a favourite, they can describe the last time they ate out.

Vocabulary

1 Point out the examples and do another one to show that the students can use more than one adjective with each photo.

> **Suggestions**
> Jumbo: busy; famous; popular; big
> McDonald's: busy; famous; popular; quick; big; cheap
> Solo per Due: comfortable; romantic; friendly; quiet; slow; small

2 📼 Do one with the whole class as an example before students complete the activity individually. Do not give feedback yet.
- Play the recording for students to check their answers.
- You could play the recording again and ask students to repeat the adjectives chorally and individually to help students say them with the correct stress.

> ■ ▪: famous; busy; quiet; friendly
> ■ ▪ ▪: comfortable; popular
> ▪ ■ ▪: romantic; expensive

Reading

3 Students should write the name of the restaurant above the correct review. Students check their answers to Exercise 3 before whole class feedback.

> 1 McDonald's   2 Solo per Due   3 Jumbo

- You can extend this activity by asking students to describe restaurants or cafés in the locality, using the adjectives in Exercise 1. This can be done as a whole class activity.

Grammar focus

4 Students read the restaurant reviews in Exercise 3 again to help them finish the table with the correct spelling.
- Use examples from the text to help the students with the stress in superlative sentences, for example:
  the most famous restaurant in Hong Kong
  the smallest restaurant in the world.
- If the students have problems pronouncing superlative sentences because of the different parts, be ready to break them down into smaller parts and backchain.

	Adjective	Superlative
1 syllable	old	the oldest
	small	the smallest
	quick	the quickest
	cheap	the cheapest
	big	the biggest
Ends with 'y'	noisy	the noisiest
	busy	the busiest
	friendly	the friendliest
2 syllables or more	comfortable	the most comfortable
	famous	the most famous
	romantic	the most romantic
	popular	the most popular
Irregular	good	the best
	bad	the worst

Practice

5 Do the first one as an example with the whole class.

> 1 the best   2 the most famous   3 the most romantic
> 4 the most expensive   5 the cheapest   6 the most popular   7 the most comfortable   8 the busiest

6 Students work in pairs to compare the restaurants using the information in the table.
- Go round, monitoring, and noting any errors in superlative forms they are still making.

Get talking

7 Give students a few minutes to choose one of the restaurants from Exercise 1 that they would like to visit. Ask them to think of reasons why they want to go there.
- Divide the students into groups (of four) and explain that they need to agree on the same restaurant to go to.
- Hold whole class feedback in which one member of each group tells the rest of the class which restaurant they chose and why.
- Alternatively, you could personalise the lesson more by asking the students to choose from three well-known restaurants in their area.
- You could also vary the activity by changing the size of the groups. By setting up a pyramid discussion and getting the students to decide individually and then in pairs and then in threes and then in larger groups, you will give the students more speaking practice.

Vocabulary   Telephones
Function   Telephoning
Language to go   Taking and leaving messages

On the phone

Language notes

- Different languages have different telephoning conventions. Common mistakes include answering by saying:
  I am Simon. [*This is*]
- The students are introduced to some phrasal verbs in this lesson. Students will need to know that in expressions such as *call me back* and *put me through*, the pronoun must be between the verb and the particle. Common mistakes include:
  Can you tell him to call back me? [*call me back*]

Way in

- Write or dictate these four questions.
  How many phones do you have at home?
  How often do you use the phone?
  Do you make personal calls at work?
  What's your longest phone call?
  Give students a minute to think of their answers and then students ask and answer the questions in pairs.

Vocabulary and speaking

1 Students complete the activity in pairs. During whole class feedback, point to the individual pictures and elicit the correct word. Check students' pronunciation of the new vocabulary.

A mobile phone/cellphone   B text message
C pager   D answering machine   E area code

2 Do one with the whole class as an example before students complete the activity individually.

1 Directory Enquiries   2 put you on hold
3 take a message   4 text   5 call you back

3 Students ask and answer the questions in pairs. You may like to vary the pairs so students get the chance to work with different partners.

Extra information: These are the international codes for the UK, USA and Australia:
UK 44   Australia 61   USA 1

Reading

4 Check students know the meaning of *calling* and *answering* before they complete the activity. You could do this by miming.

Heading for 1–4: *Calling*
Heading for 5–8: *Answering*

Listening

5 📟 Point out the notepad that students have to complete and play the recording once. You may need to play the recording again if students have had problems completing the message.

Caller's Name: Tom
Message: Please call ✓   Person will call back ☐
Number: 01632 895506

Language focus

6 Students read the advice about phone etiquette in Exercise 4 again to help them finish the exercise. Point out to students that not all the pieces of advice are needed and they can use a number more than once.
- You will need to highlight the use of *This is Tom* and *It's Tom* and *call me back* not *call back me*.
- This would also be a good opportunity to focus on the pronunciation. Use the recording from Exercise 5 as a model and get students repeating the sentences chorally and individually. The expressions are long and can be tricky for the students so be ready to break them into smaller chunks.

5 Hello.
2 Hi, this is Tom. Can I speak to Sue?
6 Sorry, she isn't here at the moment. Can I take a message?
3 Yes, please. Could you ask her to call me back? It's Tom.
7 Call Tom. Has she got your number?
3 It's 01632 895506.
8 So that's 01632 895506.
4 Thanks very much. Bye.

Practice

7 Point out the example with the whole class before students complete the exercise individually. Students could compare their answers in pairs before whole class feedback.

1 she isn't   2 This is   3 Has she got   4 call me back

8 Divide the students into pairs and explain that they have different parts of the same phone conversation.
- Students look at their phone conversation and, individually complete the missing part.
- Make sure that each student's sentences are correct before you regroup the pairs to act out their conversations.
- They then work with their partner, saying the lines which they wrote, to roleplay a completely new phone conversation which they have created.

Get talking

9 Demonstrate the activity with a student in order to show them how to use the prompts in the boxes. The students then work in pairs and roleplay the conversation.
- When they have finished, students change roles and repeat the conversations to make sure they practise both sides.

Vocabulary Social etiquette
Grammar *Should* for advice
Language to go Giving advice to visitors

Culture shock

Language notes

- Students are already familiar with the modal verbs *can* and *could* so remind students of the omission of auxiliaries and *to*. Common mistakes include:
  You should ~~to~~ use first names.
- *Should* has both a strong and a weak pronunciation. (See the phonemic chart on page 12.) In sentences, the weak form of should /ʃəd/ can be difficult for the students to hear/pronounce:
  You should /ʃəd/ arrive on time.
  In negatives, questions and short answers, should /ʃʊd/ has a strong pronunciation:
  Yes, you should. /ʃʊd/
  You shouldn't /ʃʊdnt/ use first names.
  Should /ʃʊd/ I take a present?

Way in

- Introduce the topic of cultural advice by giving some cultural information about a place you know well. For example, in the UK, it is not a good idea to walk to the front of a queue.
- Alternatively, tell the students a short, simple story about a cultural misunderstanding you have made. Ask the students if they have any similar stories of cultural misunderstandings.

Vocabulary and speaking

1 Students complete the activity in pairs. During whole class feedback, point to the individual pictures and elicit the correct word. Check students can pronounce them correctly.

Suggestions
1 shake hands; arrive on time; wear a suit
2 wear a suit; bow   3 take your shoes off
4 give a present; kiss; use first names

2 Students complete Exercise 2 in pairs.

Listening

3 Encourage students to predict the answers before they listen by reading the statements and guessing the correct advice. Students then listen to see if their guesses were correct. You may need to play the recording more than once.

1 ✓   2 ✗   3 ✓   4 ✗

Grammar focus

4 Make sure you highlight the lack of auxiliary verb and *to*. You could remind students that *should* is similar in form to *can* and *could*. This will help students to see patterns in the language.

We use **should** + infinitive (without *to*) to say it's a good idea.
We use **shouldn't** + infinitive (without *to*) to say it's a bad idea.

5 The aim of the exercise is to highlight the stressed words and to show the different strong and weak pronunciations of *should*. To demonstrate the activity, write an example sentence on the board for students to identify the stressed words.
- Play the recording for students to listen and complete the activity.

1 *Should* I take a *present*?
2 *Yes*, you *should*.
3 *Should* you use *first* names?
4 *No*, you *shouldn't*.

6 Play the recording again and pause it after each expression for students to repeat chorally and individually.

Practice

7 Students should fill in the gaps with *should* and *shouldn't* and then complete the quiz in pairs. Check students know the meaning of *Muslim* before they complete the activity.
- Students can check their answers in the key on page 86 of the Students' Book to find out their score.

1 shouldn't   2 Should   3 Should   4 shouldn't
5 Should   6 shouldn't   7 shouldn't

Key: 1 b   2 b   3 b   4 a   5 a   6 a   7 b

- In whole class feedback, ask students how well they scored in the quiz, and which items surprised them, or are very different in their country.
- You could extend this, if you have time, into a class discussion of interesting/different social customs they have heard about or experienced when travelling abroad.

Get talking ...

8 Explain that students need to prepare some advice for foreign visitors. Give students five minutes to make notes for the different categories of information.
- Divide students into groups (of four) and get each student to present their advice to the group.
- At the end, have a whole class discussion on what was the most common/important/the strangest advice.

... and writing

9 Students use their ideas from Exercise 8 to write an e-mail giving advice. This can be done in class or at home.
- For an example of an e-mail, see **Writing bank** page 150.

Vocabulary   Money verbs
Function   Suggestions
Language to go   Making suggestions for social arrangements

Party time!

Language notes

- There are a number of different exponents for suggestions and their different grammatical patterns can cause problems for the students.
  Shall is used with *I* or *we* to make offers:
  Shall I/ we help you?
  Let's is followed by an infinitive without *to*:
  Let's have a party.
  How about is followed by verb + *-ing* or a noun:
  How about (having) a party?
  Common mistakes include:
  Let's ~~to~~ go to a hotel.
  How about ~~to go~~ to a restaurant? [*going*]
- Using polite intonation is another problem with making suggestions. In order to sound polite, the students need to say the expressions with a high voice range and not sound 'flat'.
- Students need to be aware of the prepositions that go with *pay*, *spend* and *buy*, for example:
  buy something for somebody
  spend money on something
  pay for something by credit card.

Way in

- Ask what makes a good party. Elicit ideas such as lots of people, nice food, good music, something to drink, a nice place. If students are interested, get them to tell you about the best or worst parties they have been to.

Speaking and vocabulary

1   Students answer the four questions about parties in pairs. Hold whole class feedback to listen to a few of the students' answers.

> Picture 1: a fancy dress party
> Picture 2: a leaving party
> Picture 3: a birthday party

2   Make sure students understand that they have to do two tasks – to match the verbs to the sentences and then to complete those sentences. Point out the example and students then complete the activity in pairs.

- Go round the class monitoring. If some pairs of students are having problems, you could guide them to the answers.
- Tell students to put their pens down and read aloud the correct answers but do not let the students write anything. When you have finished all the sentences, students then complete the exercise from memory.

> 1 b   2 c   3 d   4 a   5 f   6 e

Listening

3   Focus students' attention on the picture and elicit who the people are. Students then read the information in the box and guess what the client and the party organiser talk about, before listening to the recording to check their predictions.

> drinks ✓;   place ✓;   music ✓;   date of party ✗;
> number of guests ✗;   food ✓

4   Play the recording again for students to check their answers in pairs before whole class feedback.

> 1 the office   2 wine   3 karaoke

Language focus

5   It would be a good idea to put the sentences on the board to make it easier to highlight the different grammatical patterns. Show students that *shall* and *let's* are followed by the infinitive without *to* and that *How about* is followed by a verb + *-ing* or a noun. Then focus on the responses for accepting and rejecting suggestions.

6a   The aim of the exercise is to highlight the stressed words and to reinforce the polite intonation. Play the recording and pause it after each expression. Students repeat the expressions chorally and then individually.

6b   Practise the first suggestion with the whole class before students complete the activity individually.

Practice

7   Students can complete the exercise individually or in pairs before whole class feedback.

> 1 go; have; inviting; that's   2 have; getting; ask

8   Divide students into pairs to practise the dialogues.

Get talking

9   As a whole class, decide what type of party you are going to organise. Use the suggestion in the coursebook or adapt it to include a school or fancy dress party.

- Explain that students must work in groups (of four) to discuss the different information in the table in order to organise a party under the £500 budget. Students then present their ideas to the whole class.
- Depending on the interests of your class, you could add a competitive element and have the students vote on which group organised the best party.

Vocabulary Movies
Grammar *Say* and *tell*
Language to go Talking about movies

At the movies

Language notes

- Students need to be aware that *tell* is always followed by a direct object and that *say* can be followed by an indirect object:
  He said (to her) he likes science fiction films.
  She told him she likes action films.
  This lesson focuses on the verb patterns in reported speech and presents the present tense in direct speech changing to the past tense in indirect speech.
- Note the difference between US and UK English.
  film, cinema (UK) = movie, movie theater (US)

Way in

- Think of a well-known film that all the students will know in English. Play 'Hangman' on the board with the name of the film (for example, *Jurassic Park*). Write a short line to represent each letter of the name of the film.
- Ask students to guess a letter which appears in the name. If a student guesses correctly, write the letter in. For example:
  J _ _ A _ _ _ _ _ _ A _ K
- If a student chooses a letter which doesn't appear in the name, write the letter on the board and draw one part of the 'hangman'. If the students make twelve incorrect guesses the 'hangman' is completed and the teacher wins. For example:
  X T Y O G L
  V F D E B M

- You could then get students to think of other films and take it in turns to play the game.

Vocabulary and speaking

1 Give students a minute or so to work out their answers and then do this as a whole class activity. Point to the photos and elicit the correct phrase.
  - The pictures are from the films *The World Is Not Enough* (A), *Star Wars* (B), *Mr Bean – The Movie* (C) and *Casablanca* (D).

1 D   2 A   3 B   4 C

Extra information: Picture A: *The World Is Not Enough* (1999 – directed by Michael Apted) stars Pierce Brosnan in his third Bond movie alongside Sophie Marceau. It features one of the longest and most exciting opening credits with a speedboat chase up the River Thames. Picture B: *Star Wars* (1977 – directed by George Lucas) starring Harrison Ford, Mark Hamill, Alec Guinness and Carrie Fisher, is one of the most popular and profitable science fiction films ever. It was famous for its advanced use of special effects and won six Academy Awards. Picture C: *Mr Bean – The Movie* (1997 – directed by Mel Smith) is called 'the ultimate disaster movie'. It is a feature length version of the comedy TV series, which follows the misadventures of Mr Bean. Starring Rowan Atkinson, *Mr Bean – The Movie* sees the helpless character travel to Los Angeles to protect the American masterpiece 'Whistler's Grandmother' with disastrous consequences.

Picture D: *Casablanca* (1942 – directed by Michael Curtiz) starring Ingrid Bergmann and Humphrey Bogart, is the classic black and white romantic story of two men fighting for the same woman's love. Set in Morocco during World War II, much of the film takes place in Rick's Bar.

2 Say the words and get students to tell you the number(s) of the photo in which they can be seen.

1 A; B; C; D   2 D   3 A   4 A

3 This activity is designed to introduce the topic and practise the new vocabulary. Divide the students into pairs to ask and answer the questions.

Reading

4 Students read the questions through before reading the article and completing the activity.

1 *Star Wars*.   2 The special effects.   3 *Dr No*.
4 The actor.   5 *Casablanca*.   6 The story.

Grammar focus

5 Give students a minute to work out the rules before whole class feedback. Highlight the optional use of *that* and the irregular past form of *say* and *tell*. Point out the back-shift tense change from present simple in direct speech to past simple in reported speech.

1 say   2 tell   3 past

Practice

6 Students complete this exercise individually then check the answers in whole class feedback.

1 said; loved   2 told; was   3 said; was   4 told; liked
5 said; was   6 told; were

Get talking ...

7 Give students a few minutes to make notes on their favourite film. If you think students will have problems coming up with ideas, have a quick brainstorm of famous films.
  - Circulate to help students with vocabulary they ask for.

8 Divide the students into groups (of three) to discuss their favourite films. Students then form new groups of three to discuss who liked which film and why.
  - You could make this more realistic by suggesting that students need to decide on a film to watch together as a class.
  - Students make notes on their individual choice before forming groups to discuss and agree on one film for the whole group. Then the groups present their choices to the class.

... and writing

9 Depending on time, this could be done in class or for homework.
  - For an example of a review of a film or place, see **Writing bank** page 148.

Vocabulary   Restaurant words
Grammar   *Would like/like, would prefer/prefer*
Language to go   Ordering food and drink in a restaurant

Would you like the menu?

Language notes

- Although students can understand the difference in meaning between a general liking/preference and a specific request, they often make mistakes of form. Common mistakes when asking or expressing preference are:
  ~~Do~~ you like dessert? [*Would*]
  ~~I prefer~~ the salmon, please. [*I'd prefer*]
  ~~You like~~ some coffee? [*Would you like*]
- This is the first time students have seen the modal verb *would* and it is necessary to highlight the contraction (*'d*) and the short answer form (*Yes, I would.*):
  A: *I'd like a coffee. Would you like one?*
  B: *Yes, I would.*

Way in

- Draw a menu on the board and split it into three areas for the starters, main course and dessert. Do not write these words yet but brainstorm food vocabulary for each category.

Speaking and vocabulary

1   Students discuss the questions in pairs, then hold some quick whole class feedback.

2   Elicit some examples before students continue the activity in pairs, for example: *There are some knives in picture 4. There aren't any spoons*. During feedback, point to the items in the picture and elicit the words from the students.
   - This would be a good opportunity to check the pronunciation of any words the students mispronounce. You could do this by modelling the words and then getting the students to repeat them chorally and individually.

3   Depending on your students, this activity could be done individually or in pairs.

1 main course   2 side dish   3 dessert   4 bill
5 house red/white

Listening

4   This exercise has been designed to help students ask about dishes whose description on the menu they do not understand. This is a common problem for learners at this level.
   - Explain that students must tick the 'Simple Salmon' menu and wine list to complete Exercise 4. Play the recording for students to listen and complete the activity.

Salmon Ritz ✓   Salmon Savoy ✓
House red ✓   Mixed salad ✓

5   Play the recording again for students to match the dishes with the ingredients. You may need to play this more than once.

1 b   2 c   3 a

Grammar focus

6   First point out the key, to explain what *a* and *b* represent. Then students decide if each sentence is an *a* type (what you usually like) or a *b* type (what you want now/in the future).

1 a; a   2 a; a   3 b; b   4 b; b

Practice

7a   The aim of this activity is to develop the students' ability to recognise the subtle difference between the two forms of the verb.
   - Play the recording and pause it after each expression for the students to complete the activity.

1 b   2 a   3 b

7b   This would be a good opportunity to get students saying the sentences. You can use the recording as a model or say the sentences yourself. Ask students to repeat the expressions chorally and then individually and check their pronunciation.

8   Students complete this exercise individually, then check their answers in whole class feedback.

1 b   2 b   3 a   4 a

9   Students do this activity in pairs. They should write out the conversation first, then practise saying it in pairs.
   - Go round the class checking that they are using *would* correctly.

Suggestions:
A: Are you ready to order?
B: Yes, I'd like the salmon, please.
A: Would you like a starter?
B: No, thank you.
A: What would you like to drink?
B: A bottle of the house white, please.
A: Would you like dessert?
B: No, thank you. The bill, please.

Get talking

10   Divide the students into groups (of three) and explain that student A is the waiter and student B and C are the customers.
   - Make the roleplay as realistic as possible by reorganising the tables and encouraging the students to take on roles to add to the motivation.
   - Students then roleplay a conversation using the menu on page 88. Make sure students change roles so each group member is both a customer and a waiter.

LESSON 35

Vocabulary Practical activities
Grammar Present perfect for experience
Language to go Asking people about their practical experience

Island life

Language notes

- Students often have problems with the present perfect because other languages have a verb with a similar form (*have* + past participle) but a different meaning.
  In English, the present perfect is used to describe an action which happened at an indefinite time in the past. Common mistakes include:
  He ~~has~~ lived abroad last year.
  ~~Did you ever teach~~ children? [*Have you ever taught*]
- Students find the difference between *They've been to …* and *They've gone to …* difficult to grasp. Highlight the fact that *They've been to …* means 'gone and come back'.
  He's gone to India. (He's still in India.)
  He's been to India. (He went at some time in the past, but he isn't there now.)
- The present perfect consists of the auxiliary verb *have* and the past participle. Although students are familiar with *have* as an auxiliary verb, the combination of the auxiliary *have/has* and the past participle *had* can confuse students:
  Have you had a good holiday?
  Other mistakes include inserting the auxiliary *do*:
  ~~Do you have lived~~ abroad? [*Have you lived*]
- There are also a large number of irregular past participles that the students have to learn. Show them where the list is in the Phrasebook.

Way in

- Ask what their favourite/least favourite TV programmes are. Brainstorm the names of famous TV programmes that involve the general public. This should elicit different types of quiz shows and interactive TV along the lines of *Survivor* in the USA and *Big Brother* in the UK and Europe.

Speaking and vocabulary

1 Point out the photo of the island and then divide the students into pairs to discuss with their partner.
2 Focus students' attention on the advert and ask 'Where is it from?'. Elicit a newspaper or magazine. Ask and answer the questions about it as a whole class activity.

> 1 30 people to live on the island for a year.

3 Students then work in pairs to complete Exercise 3.

> 1 b 2 a 3 d 4 c

4 Depending on your students, this activity could be done individually or in pairs. Check the answers with the whole class.

> 1 c 2 d 3 b 4 a

Reading

5 Make sure students know that Andrew Ho is an applicant for the Adventure TV show in the ad. Students complete Exercise 5 individually by ticking the correct boxes on the application form.

> 1 Yes ✓ 2 No ✓ 3 Yes ✓

- For an example of form filling, see **Writing bank** page 146.

Grammar focus

6a This is a difficult concept for the students to understand so you may want to write the sentences on the board and ask the grammar questions to the whole class.

> 1 Is he teaching adults now? *no*
> 2 Do we know exactly when he taught adults? *no*
> (The present perfect tense in the sentence *I've taught adults…* places emphasis on the experience, not on the exact time it happened.)

- If you have time, you could quickly practise the pronunciation of the example sentences.

6b Students complete the rules in pairs.

> 1 We use the present perfect to talk about experience when the time *is not* important.
> 2 We make the present perfect with *have* or *has* + past participle.

Practice

7 Depending on the class, the students can do this activity in pairs or individually.
- When checking the answers with the whole class make it clear where contractions are/aren't acceptable.

> 1 Have; written; have   2 Has; taught; hasn't; 's/has looked after   3 Have; looked after; haven't   4 Have; played; have; 've/have played   5 Has; grown; has

Get talking

8 Explain that students are going to interview each other to see who is a suitable candidate to go to the island. After completing the 'you' column, students form groups of three to conduct the interview. For feedback, discuss who were the most suitable people in the class to live in Mulkinney.
- Alternatively, you could move away from the island theme and ask the students to adapt/make a new form for interviewing a candidate for a job or a flat/house.
- Encourage the students to make the interview as realistic as possible by using greetings and personal questions outside the target language. Reorganising the seating and asking the students to act out roles can help with this.
- To extend this activity you could ask students to write a letter of application to 'Adventure TV'.
  For an example of a formal letter, see **Writing bank** page 152.

Vocabulary Activities at work
Grammar *Have to/don't have to*
Language to go Describing jobs

Hard work

Language notes

- Students have problems with the meaning of *don't have to*. Many languages have the same form but use it to express an obligation *not* to do something. In English, *don't have to* expresses a lack of obligation and *mustn't* expresses a negative obligation. For example:
  *I **don't have to** go to school today because it's a holiday.* (lack of obligation)
  *I **mustn't** be late for the meeting.* (obligation not to)
- Students sometimes have problems with the different sounds of the verb *have* and the weak form of *to*, for example: *I have /hæv/ to /tə/ work long hours.*
- The short answer for the 'yes/no' question with *have to* is *Yes, I do.* not *Yes, I have*:
  Do you have to work late?
  Yes, I ~~have~~. [do]

Way in

- Brainstorm a list of jobs. Say a place where people work and elicit the names of jobs of people who work there. Examples of places you could use are: *school, hospital, court, government, factory.*

Vocabulary and speaking

1 Students ask and answer the question in pairs.
  You can then hold a quick feedback session with the whole class.

2 Students read the texts and complete the sentences. It is a good idea to encourage students to read the whole text to get a general idea of the content before completing it.
  - Do the first one with the whole class as an example before students complete the exercise in pairs.

  1 work in a team   2 arrange meetings
  3 drive to work   4 travel   5 give presentations
  6 meeting clients   7 work long hours
  8 serve customers   9 make decisions

3 Students discuss Exercise 2 in pairs.

Reading

4 Students look at the photo of Marcus and predict which activities he does in his job. You can do this as a whole class activity. Students don't read the text yet.

5 Students read the article and check their answers to Exercise 4.

  work long hours; drive; serve customers; work in a team

  - Check that students understand *company* and *tips* from the article as useful vocabulary when discussing different jobs.

Grammar focus

6 Make sure students know the meaning of *necessary* before you ask them to complete the rules. Get students to give you a couple more examples to check they have understood the meaning and form.

  1 We use *have to* (or *has to*) + infinitive when something **is** necessary.
  2 We use *don't/doesn't have to* + infinitive when something **isn't** necessary.

7 ▣ Play the recording and pause it after each expression for students to repeat the model chorally and individually. Point out the weak form of *to /tə/*.

Practice

8 Point out the example and then students complete the exercise individually.
  - Check the answers with the whole class.

  1 We have to meet clients.
  2 I don't have to serve customers.
  3 What does your boss have to do?
  4 He has to give presentations.
  5 Do you have to travel? Yes, I do.
  6 Do you have to work in a team? No, I don't.
  7 They don't have to work long hours.
  8 Do you have to wear a suit?

Get talking

9 Tell each student to add one more job to the list and give them a couple of minutes to make notes on the activities in the two categories.
  - Briefly, hold whole class feedback to elicit some of the activities people have to/don't have to do in these jobs.

10 Organise the students into groups of four and explain that, as a group, they need to decide on the same sixth job. Students then rank the jobs in order of best to worst.
  - When each group has decided on an order, they must tell the whole class their decision and the reasons why. Depending on the class, you could extend this into a class discussion.

LESSON 37

Vocabulary Parts of the body; illnesses
Function Making and accepting apologies
Language to go Making excuses

Excuses, excuses

Language notes

- Students need to be aware that it is common to give a reason after the apology, for example:
  I'm afraid I can't come to work because I've got a cold.
- Students often sound rude because of their flat intonation. English speakers use a high voice range in order to sound polite.
- The pronunciation of the following words sometimes causes difficulties for students:
  cough /kɒf/
  sore throat /sɔː θrəʊt/
  stomachache /stʌməkeɪk/
  headache /hedeɪk/
  temperature /tempərətʃə/

Way in

- Play 'Hangman' with the word *excuses*. (See Way in section in Lesson 33 for how to play 'Hangman'.)
- Check students understand the meaning of *excuses* by giving them a situation where you have made an excuse. Then brainstorm different situations where people give excuses. For example, you didn't do your homework, you're late, you don't want to do something. If you have a strong class, elicit some excuses they have used at work or at school (for example, *The dog ate my homework.* or *I left it on the bus.*)

Vocabulary and speaking

1 Do the first one as an example with the whole class before students complete the activity in pairs.

> 1 eye 2 back 3 hand 4 arm 5 head 6 nose
> 7 mouth 8 stomach 9 ear 10 throat 11 leg
> 12 foot

2 Students work in pairs to practise the names of parts of the body.

3 Students do this exercise in pairs or individually, depending on your class.

> 1 C 2 A 3 B 4 B 5 A 6 B 7 C

4 Play the recording of sound effects, pause after the first one and elicit the illness / problem from the whole class. Then split the class into pairs. Play the recording of the other sound effects one by one, pausing and giving students time to tell their partner the problem. Be ready to go back and correct any problems.

> 1 He's got a cold.
> 2 She's got a temperature.
> 3 He's got a cough.
> 4 She's hurt her hand.
> 5 He's got a headache.

5 Students work in pairs to test each other. Quick student–student tests can be very effective at helping the students memorise the vocabulary, but keep the pace up to motivate the students.

Listening

6 It is crucial that students understand that Tony is not really ill. He is making excuses and can't come to work because he is actually on holiday. Use the picture of Tony and his boss to elicit where they are.

- Play the recording and pause it after the first excuse. Make sure students agree on the correct answer and then play the recording to the end before giving whole class feedback.

> 1 He's got a cough.
> 2 He's got a cold.
> 3 He's got a stomachache.
> 4 He's hurt his back.

Language focus

7 Students complete the table individually before whole class feedback. Check students have understood by eliciting different examples using the same patterns, for example:
I'm sorry, but I've got a stomachache.

- Alternatively, you could do this briefly in open pairs.

> **Apology:**
> I'm really sorry, but
> *I'm afraid*
> **Explanation:**
> *I've got a headache.*
> I've got a temperature.
> **Accept apology:**
> Don't worry!
> *That's OK.*
> *What a pity!*

8 This exercise focuses on stress and intonation. Play the recording and pause it after each expression for students to repeat the model chorally and individually.

- Make sure that the students have a high voice range by making the students exaggerate. Although this may sound unnatural to them, it will help students come close to natural speech in English.

Practice

9 Students do this in pairs.

> 1 b 2 d 3 c 4 e 5 a

Get talking

10 Explain that students are going to make and accept some excuses. Demonstrate the activity with one student in the class before dividing them into As and Bs.

- Each student uses their prompts to make and accept the appropriate excuses. If you have a strong class, you could encourage them to expand the dialogues and refuse to accept the excuse.

LESSON 38

Vocabulary World issues
Grammar *Will* for predictions
Language to go Making predictions

Big issues

Language notes

- Students need to be aware that *will* is not the only way of expressing the future in English. The present continuous and *going to* are also used for future references.
- Although students should be familiar with the affirmative form of *will* because it has been introduced functionally in the context of spontaneous decisions, this lesson focuses on *will* to express future prediction.
- The students often have problems with pronouncing the contraction *I'll* /aɪl/.
- Expressing negative predictions with the verb *think* often causes problems for students. The first verb (*think*) takes the negative. For example:
  I think we won't live in space. [*I don't think we'll*]

Way in

- Set the scene and revise dates by eliciting the day's date and the year. Then dictate five or six future dates and years (for example, *25 December 2015, 3/5/2050, August 2009*). During whole class feedback, revise the different ways of writing dates.
- If you have a strong class you could ask them to make some predictions about the dates. This will test to see if the students can use *will* for future predictions.

Vocabulary and speaking

1 Do the first one as an example with the whole class before students complete the activity in pairs.

1 b 2 d 3 e 4 g 5 a 6 f 7 c

2 Students work in pairs to match the words from Exercise 1 with the photos.

1 F 2 G 3 B 4 A 5 D 6 C 7 E

3a Point out the example and ask students to complete the activity in pairs.
- Note that communication can be stressed in two different ways: *communication* or *communication*.

politics; transport; space; climate; population; economy; communication

3b Students listen to the recording to check their answers.

4 Students discuss this in pairs. Use whole class feedback as an opportunity for a quick discussion about the changes.

Reading

5 Part of the interest in the website text comes from the fact that Clarke made these predictions in 1967 about the year 2000. You could highlight this by writing the two years on the board. Point out the first prediction made in 1967 about the year 2000 and ask students if it is true now. Then students complete the activity in pairs.

1 True 2 True and false (we have newspapers on computers, but we still use paper). 3 True 4 False
5 True that the population has increased to 6 billion.
6 False (not everyone) 7 False 8 True 9 False

Extra information: *Arthur C Clarke* is an English scientist and science fiction writer whose fictional ideas have closely mirrored real life, particularly in the development of space and satellite communications. Born in the UK and now living in Sri Lanka, Clarke is best known for his writing and collaboration on Stanley Kubrick's film *2001: Space Odyssey*.

Grammar focus

6a Divide this activity into stages. Refer students back to the website predictions to help them complete 1–3.

1 We *will* go on holiday in space.
2 People *won't* live in cities.
3 What *will* happen in the future?

6b When students have completed part a) of the exercise they can complete the rule.

We use *will* (*not*) + infinitive (without *to*) to make predictions about the future.

6c Let students say the sentences and decide which is more natural (sentence b). Explain that this is how we make negative predictions with *think* and *will*.

7 This exercise focuses on recognising and producing the contractions. Play the recording and pause it after each word to give them time to choose. When students have finished, hold whole class feedback.
- Then play the recording again, pausing after each one for students to repeat chorally and individually. (See the phonemic chart on page 12.)

1 b 2 a 3 a 4 b

Practice

8 Students do this exercise in pairs. If you have time, use feedback as an opportunity to work on pronunciation.

1 Where will people go on holiday?
2 I don't think people will go on holiday in space.
3 Do you think computers will listen to instructions?
4 I think everyone will speak English.
5 The climate in the UK won't/will not be hotter.
6 Do you think technology will cost less?
7 I think transport will be cheaper.
8 The world economy will be stronger.

Get talking

9 Divide the students into groups of four and explain that each group must make predictions for the year 2050.
- When they have finished, reorganise the groups and tell them to exchange their groups' predictions.
- Depending on your class, you could then expand this into a whole class discussion about general and more personal future predictions.

Vocabulary Expressions of time with *for* and *since*
Grammar Present perfect: how *long/for/since*
Language to go Talking about how long people do things for

Long life

Language notes

- Although students are familiar with the present perfect used to express indefinite time, this lesson focuses on the present perfect to talk about unfinished actions that started in the past and continue in the present. Students often have problems with this because some languages use a present tense to express the same concept.
- Although the concepts of *for* and *since* are clear, students often make mistakes because of the variety of time expressions that can follow them. Be prepared to spend time on correction and consolidation.
- Students often have problems pronouncing the *-ed* ending of regular past participles.

Way in

- Think of how long you have done a number of activities, for example, been a teacher, lived in your house, studied a language. Try and get a range of large and small numbers (*20 years, two months*) Write the number of years and the activities on the board for students to guess which activity goes with which number.

Speaking and vocabulary

1. Focus students' attention on the photos in the article and ask the first question to the whole class. Students ask and answer questions 2–3 in pairs.
2. Do the first one as an example before students finish the activity individually.

   1 d   2 a   3 e   4 b   5 c

3. Do this as a whole class activity. You may like to draw a diagram like the one below to illustrate the difference in meaning between a point and a period. (You can use different months to make the meaning real for your situation.)

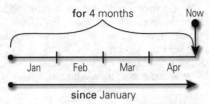

for 4 months | Now

Jan   Feb   Mar   Apr

since January

   1 New Year's Day; midday; 1st January; twelve noon
   2 over ten years; ages; a couple of months; two months; more than ten years; a long time

Reading

4. Point to the photos and the boxes and demonstrate with your finger possible ways of matching the names, jobs and ages. Students read the article and complete the activity individually.

   Dodo – tennis player – 86 years old
   Carmen – model – 70 years old
   Omara – singer – 72 years old

Grammar focus

5a. Write the example sentence on the board and ask questions 1 and 2 orally. Remind students about the contractions and negative forms of the present perfect (for example, *she's played* and *she hasn't played*).

   1 70 years ago   2 Yes

5b. Students look at the article again to find examples of the present perfect. Check students have understood the meaning by asking them to make new sentences about themselves.

   She has been a model since she was 13.
   She has sung in clubs and cabarets for over 50 years.

5c. Students read the examples and complete the rules.

   1 We use *for* with a period of time.
   2 We use *since* with a point in time.

   - If you have time, this would be a good opportunity to practise pronunciation. You could model the example sentences and get students to repeat them chorally and individually. Check students are aware of the weak pronunciation of *for* in connected speech: *For /fə/ seventy years.*

Practice

6. Students do this in pairs. Accept contractions or full forms in the answers.

   1 He's / He has taught football for 48 years.
   2 I've / I have played jazz since 1950.
   3 I've / I have had a dog since 2001.
   4 He's / He has danced since he was twelve.
   5 She's / She has painted for two years.
   6 She's / She has worked there since 10 January.
   7 We've / We have studied English since last year.
   8 They've / They have lived in Australia for eight years.

Get talking …

7. Give students a minute or two to finish the table about themselves. If students want to add more categories, let them.
   - Check students can make questions using the present simple and present perfect by demonstrating the activity (see the example). Then divide the students into pairs for the interview.
   - Remind the students to keep notes on their partner's answers, as they will need these for the writing follow up.

… and writing

8. Depending on time, this can be done in class or for homework.
   - It can be motivating for students to produce class biographies so you could set this up as a mini class project. Once the articles have been corrected and rewritten, reproduce them in a booklet to give to the students, complete with photos.
   - Alternatively, these could be compiled on a student website if students wish.

LESSON 40

Vocabulary   Work
Grammar   Giving opinions, agreeing and disagreeing
Language to go   Discussing what makes a good job

The perfect job

Language notes

- Students often have problems with the verb *agree*. In English, *agree* does not take the auxiliary *be*. In the negative, there is no difference in meaning between *do not agree* or *disagree*. Common mistakes include: I ~~am not~~ agree. [*don't*]
- Students sometimes sound bored or rude when giving opinions and disagreeing because they stress each word equally and their intonation is too flat. Encourage students to exaggerate their intonation if you find this is a problem.

Way in

- Students describe the place where they work or study. Demonstrate the activity by describing the place where you work. Talk about the room, the facilities, what you like and don't like about it. Once you have provided a model, give the students a minute to think of a place to talk about and then put them in pairs to describe it to their partner.

Speaking

1 Focus students' attention on the pictures. Students ask and answer the questions in pairs.

Reading

2 Check students know the meaning of *Internet dating agency* (a website for people to find new boyfriends/girlfriends). Students can do the exercise individually, then compare answers in pairs before whole class feedback.

> 1 British Airways: shopping centre; café; supermarket; gym   2 Somerfield: dating agency   3 Saatchi & Saatchi: pub

Vocabulary

3 Do the first one as an example before students finish the exercise in pairs.

> 1 d   2 f   3 e   4 g   5 a   6 c   7 b

Listening

4 📖 Ask students to predict the answers as a whole class activity before they listen to the recording. Depending on your class, you may need to play the recording more than once.

> 1 Manager   2 Psychologist   3 Psychologist
> 4 Manager   5 Manager

Language focus

5 Check students know the meaning of *agree*, *disagree* and *opinion* before they complete the headings in the table. You could work on the stress and intonation of the exponents here.

> The headings for the table (from top to bottom) are:
> Asking for opinion
> Giving opinion
> Agreeing
> Disagreeing

- Ask students to turn to the recording script for Exercise 4, on page 124 of the Students' Book and underline all the examples they can find of language used for *giving opinions*, *asking for opinions*, *agreeing* and *disagreeing*.
- Find the first example with the whole class before asking the students to finish the exercise individually. Do the feedback orally or via an OHP to save time.

> PRESENTER: With us today we have Nina Hooper, a professor of psychology …
> PSYCHOLOGIST: Hello.
> PRESENTER: … and Matt King, a manager of an advertising company …
> MANAGER: Hello.
> PRESENTER: Matt King, as a manager, what do you think is the most important thing for the perfect job? <u>Do you agree</u> that it's still money?
> MANAGER: No, <u>I don't think so</u>. A lot of bosses are making offices like homes. They have sofas, cafés, crèches … and I think people work hard when they feel relaxed.
> PSYCHOLOGIST: <u>Yes, but</u> some companies are doing too much. For example, <u>I think</u> a dating agency in the office is crazy! <u>I don't think</u> office relationships work.
> MANAGER: <u>That's true</u>.
> PSYCHOLOGIST: <u>In my opinion</u>, employees still want a high salary and a good pension when they retire. That's more important than games rooms and bars at work. Employees do like a good working environment, of course, but at the end of the day, they want the money.
> MANAGER: <u>No, I disagree</u>. The employees I talk to all say the most important things are friendly colleagues and a good boss.
> PSYCHOLOGIST: Let's agree to disagree on that!

Practice

6 Students work in pairs to complete the dialogues. Get students to read the whole text for the gist before they complete the exercise with one word for each gap.

> 1 but   2 my opinion; That's   3 think; I don't
> 4 agree; I don't think so   5 think; What; think
> 6 disagree

Get talking

7 As it is the last lesson of the coursebook, organise a discussion which will demonstrate how much progress the students have made. Give them a few minutes to prepare their ideas before putting them into discussion groups.

- The size of the groups depends on how much practice you want the students to have. If you have enough time and numbers, you could put the students into groups of 3, then 5 and then whole class to complete stage 3.
- During whole class feedback, keep the discussion going by asking controversial questions and asking quieter students to express their opinion too.

Photocopiable material

Vocabulary	Personal information
Grammar	*To be: am, is, are*
Function	Greetings
Language to go	Introducing yourself

Business cards

Aim

To practise language used for meeting/greeting and giving personal information about name, job, nationality, interests

Materials

One business card per student
If possible, an authentic business card

Time

30 minutes

Preparation

Photocopy the worksheet and cut it up so you can give each student a business card.

Procedure

1 Ask the students what business people give to each other when they meet for the first time. If possible, show a real business card to make the activity more relevant.

2 Give each student a business card and check that the students understand the information on it. If you have more than 15 students, make more than one copy of the cards. There are some new countries. For example, the UK, Greece, France, Argentina, Hungary.

3 Pre-teach *Could you say that again, please?* and *How do you spell it?*

4 The students must then mingle and introduce themselves in order to find people who are similar to them. Demonstrate the activity with a student by introducing yourself to them. *My name's ... Nice to meet you ... I'm ... and I'm interested in ...* . Ask the class if you and the student are similar or not. If not, repeat the demonstration until you find a student who is similar to you.

5 Ask the students to stand up and introduce themselves to the other members of the class. Encourage them to say *Could you say that again?* and *How do you spell it?* and to use the language for meeting and greeting like *Nice to meet you. How are you?* They should note the name of everyone who is similar to them.

6 Have whole class feedback. Ask the students to introduce the people in the group and say why they are similar.

Extension

Students can repeat the activity with their own personal information.

ANSWERS

Mona Lisa, Venus de Milo, David are all models/art.
Martina Hingis, David Beckham, Ronaldo are all sports people.
Marie Curie, Michaela Quinn, Bruce Banner are all doctors.
Bill Gates, George Soros and Donna Karan are all business people. Edith Piaf, Maria Callas and Yoko Ono are all artists.

Name
Mona Lisa

Place
France

Job
Model

Married / Single
Single

Interested in
Art and music

Name
Venus de Milo

Place
Italy

Job
Model

Married / Single
Married

Interested in
Sport and art

Name
David

Place
Italy

Job
Model

Married / Single
Single

Interested in
Sport and art

Name
Martina Hingis

Place
USA

Job
Tennis player

Married / Single
Single

Interested in
Sport and films

Name
David Beckham

Place
UK

Job
Football player

Married / Single
Married

Interested in
Films and sport

Name
Ronaldo da Lima

Place
Brazil

Job
Football player

Married / Single
Single

Interested in
Sport and music

Name
Marie Curie

Place
Poland

Job
Doctor

Married / Single
Married

Interested in
Music and art

Name
Michaela Quinn

Place
USA

Job
Doctor

Married / Single
Married

Interested in
Music and sport

Name
Bruce Banner

Place
USA

Job
Doctor

Married / Single
Single

Interested in
Films and sport

Name
Bill Gates

Place
USA

Job
Businessman

Married / Single
Single

Interested in
Computers

Name
George Soros

Place
Hungary

Job
Businessman

Married / Single
Single

Interested in
Art and English

Name
Donna Karan

Place
USA

Job
Businesswoman

Married / Single
Married

Interested in
Sport and music

Name
Edith Piaf

Place
France

Job
Artist

Married / Single
Married

Interested in
Art and music

Name
Maria Callas

Place
Greece

Job
Artist

Married / Single
Married

Interested in
Music and art

Name
Yoko Ono

Place
Japan

Job
Artist

Married / Single
Single

Interested in
Art and music

Vocabulary Everyday objects
Grammar Plurals; *What is/are ..?*
Language to go Asking and answering: personal information

Lottery

Aim

To practise asking for and giving personal information – *what is/ what are ...?*

Materials

One copy of the worksheet cut in half per pair. If possible, a junk mail offer to win thousands of pounds

Time

25 minutes

Preparation

Photocopy the worksheet.

Procedure

1 Set the scene by showing the students the junk mail competition 'win £££' offer or use the example in the worksheet. Tell them that they have won some money in a competition but they must phone the office and give their personal details to see how much they have won.

2 Divide the students into A and B pairs and give them the correct worksheet.

3 Demonstrate the activity with a student by asking 'What's your name? What are your initials?' and copying them in the form on the worksheet. Student A then interviews Student B and completes the form. Student A then uses the information at the bottom to decide how much their partner has won. If the student fulfils more than one category, the total prize money must be added together.

4 Tell the students to change roles and repeat the act.

5 Have class feedback and see which students won the most money.

Extension

Students can invent new information in the box which determines who wins what amount of money. They then repeat the procedure above.

Sheet A

WIN £1,000,000
£100,000
£100
£10

Phone this number and your name could win you ££££££!

Name: _____

Initials: _____

Address: _____

Email address: _____

Home and work phone numbers: _____

Surname has 5 letters = £1,000,000
Initials **M** or **P** = £100,000
Address has an '**o**' or '**u**' = £100
Phone number has a **2** or **7** = £10

Sheet B

WIN £1,000,000
£100,000
£100
£10

Phone this number and your name could win you ££££££!

Name: _____

Initials: _____

Address: _____

Email address: _____

Home and work phone numbers: _____

Surname has 9 letters = £1,000,000
Initials **J** or **S** = £100,000
Address has an '**a**' or '**i**' = £100
Phone number has a **0** or **3** = £10

Vocabulary	Nationalities and countries
Grammar	*To be* (questions and negatives)
Language to go	Asking about nationalities

Round the world quiz

Aim

To practise asking yes/no questions; revise vocabulary of countries and nationalities

Materials

One worksheet per student and one cut up country/nationality per student (If there are more than 12 students, photocopy and hand out more of the countries/nationalities.)

Time

25 minutes

Preparation

Photocopy the worksheet, one for each student. Photocopy one copy of the list of countries and nationalities. Cut up the countries and nationalities so you can give one to each student.

Procedure

1 Set the scene by asking the students about famous people and where they are from. Use famous international and national figures from cinema, politics, sport, who you think the students will know.
2 Give the students the worksheet and tell them not to write anything.
3 Then give the students a country/nationality card and tell them to find the statement it corresponds to and complete the statement. If they have problems, tell them that the number on the card corresponds to the statement.
4 Collect the country/nationality cards and check that the students have the correct answer written next to the correct question.
5 Tell students they need to stand up, mingle and ask the other students 'yes or no' questions to find the answers to all the statements. Tell them to change partners when they have got a yes answer to ensure the students mingle. Demonstrate the activity, for example, *Is* Time *English? No … Is* Time *American? Yes*. Pre-teach *Sorry, I don't know*.
6 Hold class feedback and check students have got the correct answers to the worksheet.

Extension

Divide students into groups and get them to write a similar quiz.

1 *Time* is a/an _____ magazine.

2 James Joyce and Oscar Wilde are _____ writers.

3 The word 'hamburger' is from _____ .

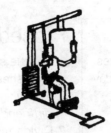

4 The word 'gym' is _____ .

5 English and _____ are the two languages in Canada.

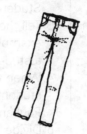

6 The word 'jeans' is _____ .

7 Vodka is from _____ and _____ .

8 La Rioja, Cordoba and Ushuaia are in _____ .

9 The word 'barbecue' is _____ .

10 Kimonos and sumo are from _____ .

11 Mah jong is a game from _____ .

12 Filipino, Spanish and _____ are the main languages in the Philippines.

1 American	2 Irish	3 Germany	4 Greek	5 French	6 Italian
7 Russia and Poland	8 Argentina	9 Spanish	10 Japan	11 China	12 English

Vocabulary   Free time activities
Grammar   Possessive adjectives and possessive 's
Language to go   Talking about people and favourite things

Blind date

Aim

To practise possessive adjectives and revise vocabulary of everyday objects and places

Materials

One copy of the worksheet cut in half per pair

Time

25 minutes

Preparation

Photocopy the worksheet and cut it in half

Procedure

1 Set the scene by showing the students the picture at the top of the worksheet and pre-teach *blind date*. You can do this by asking the following questions: *Does he have a girlfriend? No. Does he want a girlfriend? Yes. Can he see the women?*
2 Divide the class into pairs and give Student A, Worksheet A and Student B, Worksheet B. Tell them to keep their information secret.
3 Tell the students to ask questions to fill in the missing information, for example, *What's his/her favourite city?* Demonstrate the activity with a student.
4 When the students have completed the information gap, tell each student to decide for themselves who is the best blind date for Jean Paul and why.
5 Divide the students into groups of 3–4 and tell them to discuss their answers as a group. They must decide on the same person.
6 Hold class feedback where students discuss their choices and give their reasons why.

Extension

• Students take on the roles of the people on the cards and roleplay blind date with one student with their back to the class.
• Students invent new information for the characters and repeat the activity.

ANSWER KEY

Name	Jean Paul	Claire	Vanessa	Paola
Favourite city?	Rome	New York	London	Paris
Favourite food?	pizza	Italian	Chinese	French
Favourite book/writer?	George Orwell	George Orwell	Isabel Allende	Gabriel García Márquez
Favourite magazine?	*The Economist*	*Time*	*Elle*	*Newsweek*
Favourite day?	Saturday	weekend	Wednesday	Thursday

Contestant 1: Their favourite book/writer and food are the same. Their favourite magazines are *Time* and *The Economist* and their favourite day is at the weekend.

Sheet A

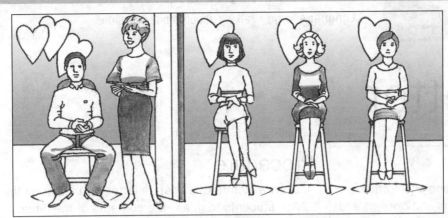

Name	Jean Paul	1 Claire	2 _____	3 Paola
Favourite city?	_____	_____	London	_____
Favourite food?	pizza	Italian	_____	French
Favourite book / writer?	_____	_____	Isabel Allende	Gabriel García Márquez
Favourite magazine?	*The Economist*	_____	_____	*Newsweek*
Favourite day?	_____	weekend	Wednesday	_____

Sheet B

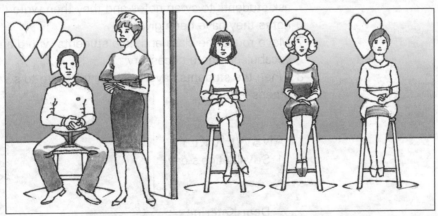

Name	_____	1 _____	2 Vanessa	3 _____
Favourite city?	Rome	New York	_____	Paris
Favourite food?	_____	_____	Chinese	_____
Favourite book / writer?	George Orwell	George Orwell	_____	_____
Favourite magazine?	_____	*Time*	*Elle*	_____
Favourite day?	Saturday	_____	_____	Thursday

Vocabulary Activities: verbs and nouns
Grammar present simple (positive)
Language to go Talking about family occasions

A letter

Aim

To practise writing an informal letter – openings and closings and making notes; present simple for talking about celebrations

Materials

One copy of the worksheet per student

Time

25 minutes

Preparation

Photocopy the worksheet.

Procedure

1 Draw a picture of a heart, a letter, and a pen on the board. Ask students to guess the contents of the letter.
2 Ask students to read the letter and decide which celebration it describes. Give feedback on the correct answer.
3 Tell the students to read the letter again and complete the gaps with the expressions from the box. Give feedback when the students have completed this.
4 The students then match the notes the writer made to the paragraphs in the original letter. Give feedback on the correct answers. As an extension to this, you could ask students to fold the page so they can only see the notes and not the original letter. Get students to rewrite the original letter from the notes given. When they have finished, ask students to compare their version with the original.
5 Ask students to think of a celebration in their country. Tell them to make notes similar to the ones in Exercise 4. You could do this note preparation stage as a whole class activity on one celebration all the students know.
6 The students then write the letter based on their notes. Alternatively, ask students to swap notes and they then write the letter for the notes they have been given.
7 Move round the class and help students with grammar and vocabulary where necessary.
8 When the students have finished, tell them to swap and read each other's letters.

ANSWER KEY
1 St Valentine's day
2

9 Malfort Road
12/02/01

Dear Katerina,
How are you? _____
_____
_____
_____
_____
_____

Write to me soon,
Love
P.S.

3 *Paragraph 1* Hi / fine / Oxford / like school + students
Paragraph 2 14th Feb / special day / give cards + presents / romantic dinner in restaurant or at home
Paragraph 3 want dinner with boyfriend / want card

1 Read the letter and fill in the gaps with the correct answer from the box. What is the celebration?

_____

_____

_____ I'm fine. I'm in Oxford at the Riverside School of English. I am here for three weeks. I like the school and especially the other students.

Next week is 14th February or St Valentine's Day. This is a special day for lovers and is an important celebration for some people in the UK. When you like someone, you buy them a card or give them a present or flowers. Some people go to restaurants and other people stay at home and cook a romantic dinner.

I want to have a romantic dinner too but my boyfriend isn't here. I hope he sends me a card!

_____

_____ Francesca

_____ My new email address is cesca@loa.com

Love from ?

xx

2 Read the letter and complete the gaps with the expressions from the box.

How are you?	Dear Katerina	Write to me soon,
Love	P.S.	9 Malfort Road 12/02/02

3 Read Francesca's notes. Match the notes to the paragraphs in the final letter.

Paragraph 1   want dinner with boyfriend / want card
Paragraph 2   Hi / fine / in Oxford / like school + students
Paragraph 3   14th Feb / special day / give cards + presents / romantic dinner in restaurant or at home

4 Write a letter to a pen friend about a special celebration in your country. Make notes as in Exercise 3.

LESSON 6

Vocabulary   Activities: verbs and nouns
Grammar   Present simple (questions and negatives)
Language to go   Talking about ways of communicating

A day at the emergency room

Aim

Present simple for habit and routine

Materials

Half the worksheet for each student

Time

25 minutes

Preparation

Photocopy the worksheet and cut in half for Student A and Student B cards

Procedure

This is a gapfill reading activity about a doctor working in an emergency room.

1 Separate students into pairs (Student A and Student B).

2 Hand out the worksheets and ask students to look at the picture and identify the job. Ask them what they think an ER doctor does, where he/she works, how much he/she works, when he/she works, etc.

3 Give students time to read through the information they have. Afterwards, explain that they need to ask their partners questions in order to find out what belongs in the gap. Choose a student to do a short illustration, for example, *When does the doctor begin work? She begins work at 6.30.* You may want to write the following prompts on the board:

When does she ...
How many ...
Who does she ...
What is ...
How does she ...
What does she ...
Where does she ...

4 When they've finished filling the gaps, quiz students on their responses.

Extension

If you wish, ask students to write down short descriptions of their jobs ... or if they are students, what they do every day. Then tell students to ask each other questions about each other's day, again, using the prompts on the board.

ANSWER KEY

The completed reading is:

I wake up, every day, at <u>five o'clock</u>. I drive my <u>car</u> to work. I work in a <u>hospital</u> in a room called the <u>ER</u>. ER means <u>emergency room</u>. I begin work at <u>6:30 am</u>. I work for <u>seven</u> hours! Sometimes, there are emergencies and I have to work <u>all day and all night</u>. After work I feel very <u>tired</u>. I work with <u>nurses</u> and other doctors. I have to take care of <u>sick</u> and injured people. I try to make them feel <u>better</u>. Sometimes I feel sleepy, so I drink a lot of <u>coffee</u>. When I have free time I find a <u>bed</u> and have a short sleep. I like my <u>job</u>, but I really like going <u>on holiday</u> too!

Sheet A

I wake up, every day, at _____ .
I drive my car to work. I work in a
_____ in a room called the ER.
ER means _____ . I begin
work at 6:30 am. I work for
_____ hours! Sometimes,
there are emergencies and I have to work all
day and all night. After work I feel very
_____ . I work with nurses and
other doctors. I have to take care of
_____ and injured people. I try
to make them feel better. Sometimes I feel
sleepy, so I drink a lot of _____ .
When I have free time I find a bed and have a
short sleep. I like my _____ ;
but I really like going on holiday too!

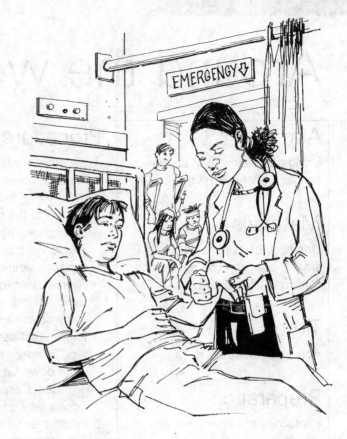

Sheet B

I wake up, every day, at five o'clock. I drive
my _____ to work. I work in a
hospital in a room called the
_____ . ER means emergency
room. I begin work at _____ .
I work for seven hours! Sometimes, there are
emergencies and I have to work
_____ . After work I feel very
tired. I work with _____ and
other doctors. I have to take care of sick and
injured people. I try to make them feel
_____ . Sometimes I feel
sleepy, so I drink a lot of coffee. When I have
free time I find a _____ and
have a short sleep. I like my job, but I really like
going _____ too!

Vocabulary   Objects you take on holiday; means of transport
Grammar   *A/an, some/any*
Language to go   Saying what you take on holiday and how you travel

Around the world

Aim

Using *a/an*, *some/any*, present simple for habit or routine

Materials

One copy of 'objects' for each small group, and one destination card for each student

Time

About 25+ minutes

Preparation

Photocopy the worksheet and cut up.

Procedure

1 Separate students into small groups of three or four. Hand out the sheet of objects. You will need to pre-teach the objects, and have them write down what each object is in the spaces provided.
2 Explain to the class that each group often goes on a trip to a specific destination. Try not to use *will* or *going to* at this point. Make sure they understand that these trips are something they do all the time (present simple). Write the four destinations on the board: *Anchorage, Alaska*; *Bangkok, Thailand*; *Stockholm, Sweden* and *Cairo, Egypt*.
3 Hand out one destination card to each group. Tell them to keep their destination secret from the other groups.
4 Explain that each group must decide what objects they take on their trip. Tell them to discuss it and come up with a list of objects. They write down what they take and what they do not take in the spaces provided. Responses should run along the lines of: *I take a passport. I don't take an umbrella. I take some sun cream.*
5 When they've finished, ask them to report back to the class. The other groups must now guess what their destination is.

Extension

You may want to ask students to compile a list of what they take when they go on holiday … in class, or for homework.

Sheet A

Sheet B

Stockholm, Sweden
When I go to Stockholm, I take
_____
_____
When I go to Stockholm, I don't take _____
_____
_____

Cairo, Egypt
When I go to Cairo, I take
_____
_____
When I go to Cairo, I don't take
_____
_____

Anchorage, Alaska
When I go to Anchorage, I take
_____
_____
When I go to Anchorage, I don't take
_____
_____

Bangkok, Thailand
When I go to Bangkok, I take
_____
_____
When I go to Bangkok, I don't take _____
_____
_____

Vocabulary Objects that people collect
Grammar *Have got*
Language to go Talking about possessions

Collectors' fair

Aim

To have
Have you got?
He's/she's got

Materials

Copy the worksheet and cut up into cards ... enough cards for at least four per person

Time

30+ minutes

Preparation

Prepare the cards.

Procedure

1 Introduce the idea of a 'collectors' fair' to the class. Ask students if they collect anything, or what types of things people collect ... you may want to write their responses on the board.

2 Hand out one card to each student. Try to have an equal number of students (preferably only one) collecting a certain object. At this point, explain that they are going to a collectors' fair ... and their card shows what they collect. To drill this point in, ask a few students 'What do you collect?' They should answer *I collect ...*
Hand out about three or four more cards to each student (depending on how much time you have). Explain that these are objects they have. Tell them they want to collect the object on their first card, so they must find out who has what they want and make an exchange.

3 As an example, ask a student 'I collect stamps. Have you got any stamps?' If they do, ask 'What do you collect?' so that the students get the idea of an exchange.

4 Ask students to stand up and mingle. When they find a person who has an object they want, they trade one of their cards for what they want. Not everyone will have what they need, so they may need to trade for something they don't want in order to get something they do want. You may want to write a few prompts on the board, such as:
I haven't got a postcard, but she's got a postcard.
I've got a coin, a postcard and a poster.
What have you got?
What do you collect?

5 The activity is finished when everyone has only the objects they collect. It's a good idea if the teacher takes part in the trading. You may want, as a final stage, to ask students questions such as: *What have you got now? Who did you get the stamps from?* etc.

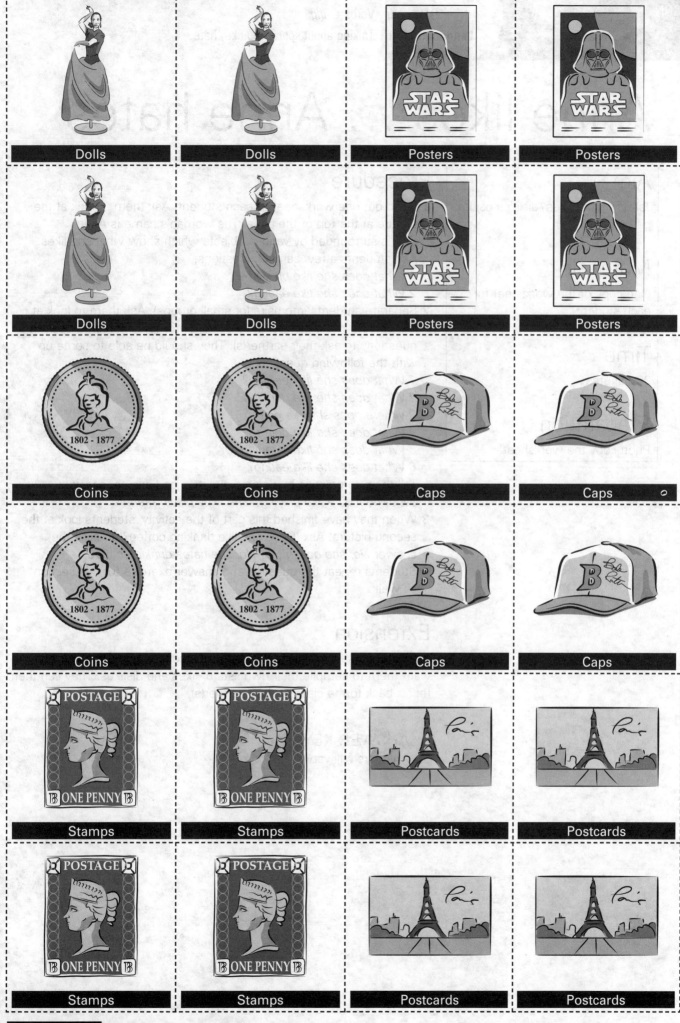

Dolls | Dolls | Posters | Posters
Dolls | Dolls | Posters | Posters
Coins | Coins | Caps | Caps
Coins | Coins | Caps | Caps
Stamps | Stamps | Postcards | Postcards
Stamps | Stamps | Postcards | Postcards

Vocabulary Sports
Grammar Verbs + *-ing*
Language to go Talking about sports you like / hate

Anne likes ... Anne hates

Aim

Talking about likes / dislikes using gerunds

Materials

One copy of the worksheet for each student

Time

30 minutes

Preparation

Photocopy the worksheet.

Procedure

1 Hand out one worksheet to each student. Ask them to look at the picture at the top of the page. The woman's name is Anne.
She is surrounded by various objects which show what she likes.
Ask students a few sample questions:
1 What does she like playing?
2 What does she like eating?

2 Separate students into pairs (or small groups). Ask them to look at the objects in the picture and the word prompts and come up with questions to ask their partner(s). They should be able to come up with the following questions:
1 What does she like playing?
2 What does she like drinking?
3 Where does she like going?
4 What does she like doing?
5 What does she like listening to?
6 What does she like eating?
Tell them to practise by doing a question and answer session:
What does she like playing? She likes playing tennis.

3 When they have finished this part of the activity, students look at the second picture. Ask 'Does she like drinking coffee?' to elicit the answer *No, she doesn't.* or *No, she hates drinking coffee.*

4 Students repeat the question and answer exercise for this section as well.

Extension

After students have finished the activities concerning 'Anne' you may want them to compile their own lists of likes and dislikes. They can then report back to the class or their partner(s).

> **ANSWER KEY**
> Answers will vary.

Anne likes …

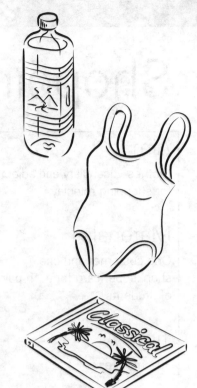

playing   drinking   going   doing   listening to   eating

_____

Anne hates …

playing   drinking   going   doing   listening to   eating

_____

Vocabulary Clothes
Function Asking for information in a shop
Language to go Shopping for clothes

Shopping for a beach party

Aim

Clothes vocabulary and adjectives for shopping roleplay

Materials

One customer and one shopkeeper card for each pair of students

Time

30+ minutes

Preparation

Two cards for each student (there will be four different cards: two customer cards and two shopkeeper cards). Make sure there are an equal number of customer / shopkeeper cards. Each student will need to have one of each.

Procedure

1 Write *beach party* on the board. Ask students what they wear to a beach party. Elicit such responses as *informal, sporty, T-shirt, jeans,* etc.

2 Separate students into pairs. Hand out the first set of cards to each pair (keep one set for later, so that students can swap roles): one student gets the customer card and the other gets the shopkeeper card. At this point, make it clear that one student is shopping and the other is selling. The cards contain a list of objects. You might want to quickly check they remember the clothes vocabulary: *T-shirt, bermuda shorts, sandals, hat, cap, sunglasses, jeans, trainers.*

3 Choose a 'customer' student and ask them what they want to buy. At this point, give a sample roleplay:
Can I help you?
Yes, I want a T-shirt.
What colour do you want?
Red.
What size do you want?
Medium.
Carry on the roleplay until students have the idea.

4 You may want to write a few prompts on the board: *size, colour, try it on, cheaper, how much.*

5 Tell the students they have £100. They are going to shop for the objects on their card, but they cannot spend more than £100. While they roleplay, make sure you monitor students, and give a few prompts where needed.
The shopkeepers will NOT have exactly what each customer is looking for. When the activity has ended, ask a few students what they bought and what they were not able to buy. Ask them how much money they spent.

6 Hand out the next set of customer/shopkeeper cards and students can swap roles, repeating the exercise.

> ### ANSWER KEY
> Answers will vary.

CUSTOMER

CARD ONE

You want:

1 a medium, red T-shirt
2 large, black sunglasses
3 a white cap
4 large blue jeans
5 medium, brown sandals

CUSTOMER

CARD TWO

You want:

1 a large, green T-shirt
2 small, red sunglasses
3 medium, brown bermuda shorts
4 large, brown hat
5 white, medium trainers

SHOPKEEPER

CARD ONE

T-shirts

| £10 | red, black | large, medium |

sunglasses

| £20 | black | small |
| £50 | black | large |

caps

| £15 | blue, white | large, medium |

jeans

| £40 | blue | medium, small |
| £50 | black | large, small |

sandals

| £35 | black, brown | large, medium, small |

SHOPKEEPER

CARD TWO

T-shirts

| £8 | blue, orange | large, medium, small |

sunglasses

| £25 | black, blue | large, small |
| £35 | red | large, medium, small |

bermuda shorts

| £25 | green, blue, brown | large, medium |

hats

| £20 | brown, yellow | large, medium |

trainers

| £50 | black | large |
| £30 | white | large, medium |

Vocabulary Adjectives to describe places in a town
Grammar *There is/are*
Language to go Talking about places you know

City guide

Aim

To practise asking questions and giving information about places with *there is/are*

Materials

One copy of the worksheet cut in half per pair

Time

25 minutes

Preparation

Photocopy the worksheet and cut in half.

Procedure

1 Ask students what they know about Edinburgh, Scotland and Dublin, Ireland. You can prompt with questions like: *What do Scotsmen wear? (kilt) What is the special beer in Ireland? (Guinness).*
2 Divide the students into A and B. Give out the information sheets and tell the students that they have different information from a website about the two places. Ask them to ask questions to complete the information.
3 Demonstrate the activity with questions like: *Are there any good places to see? things to do?* Encourage the students to use the information on the sheets, for example, *Yes, there's an old castle.*
4 Hold feedback with the class. Ask students to look at their partner's information and check they have written it correctly.

Extension

• Divide students into groups of four. Tell them they are planning to take an English course in either Dublin or Edinburgh. Ask them to discuss and choose one place they want to go to as a group and think about why. Then hold class feedback. Ask students to tell the class their choice and give their reasons, for example, *We want to go to Dublin because there is a restaurant with delicious food.*

Sheet A

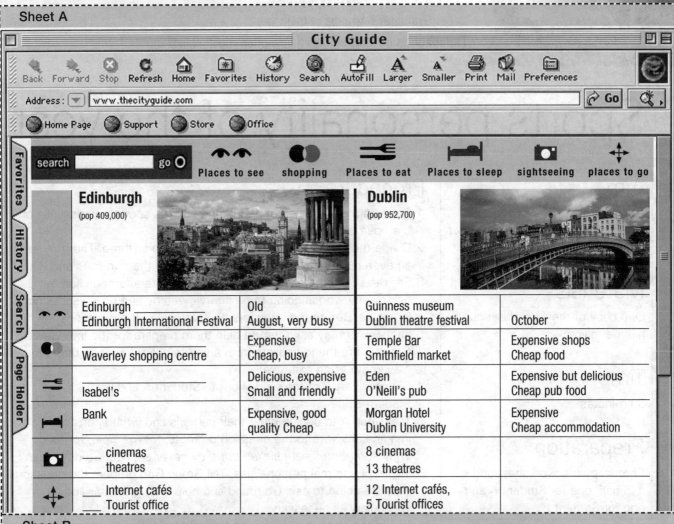

	Edinburgh (pop 409,000)		Dublin (pop 952,700)	
Places to see	Edinburgh _____ Edinburgh International Festival	Old August, very busy	Guinness museum Dublin theatre festival	October
shopping	_____ Waverley shopping centre	Expensive Cheap, busy	Temple Bar Smithfield market	Expensive shops Cheap food
Places to eat	_____ Isabel's	Delicious, expensive Small and friendly	Eden O'Neill's pub	Expensive but delicious Cheap pub food
Places to sleep	Bank _____	Expensive, good quality Cheap	Morgan Hotel Dublin University	Expensive Cheap accommodation
sightseeing	___ cinemas ___ theatres		8 cinemas 13 theatres	
places to go	___ Internet cafés ___ Tourist office		12 Internet cafés, 5 Tourist offices	

Sheet B

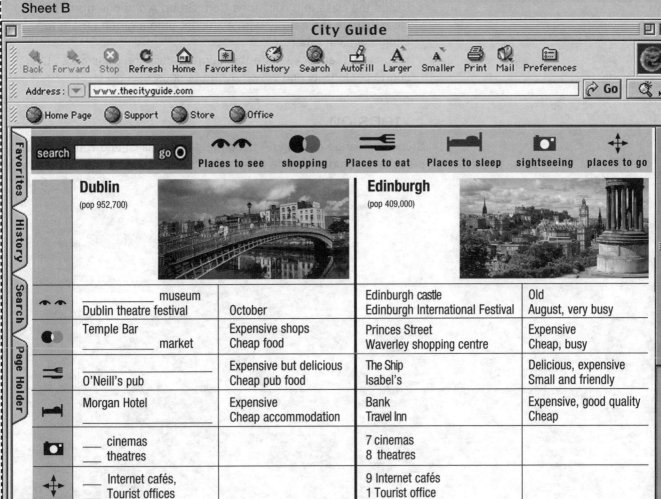

	Dublin (pop 952,700)		Edinburgh (pop 409,000)	
Places to see	_____ museum Dublin theatre festival	October	Edinburgh castle Edinburgh International Festival	Old August, very busy
shopping	Temple Bar _____ market	Expensive shops Cheap food	Princes Street Waverley shopping centre	Expensive Cheap, busy
Places to eat	_____ O'Neill's pub	Expensive but delicious Cheap pub food	The Ship Isabel's	Delicious, expensive Small and friendly
Places to sleep	Morgan Hotel _____	Expensive Cheap accommodation	Bank Travel Inn	Expensive, good quality Cheap
sightseeing	___ cinemas ___ theatres		7 cinemas 8 theatres	
places to go	___ Internet cafés, ___ Tourist offices		9 Internet cafés 1 Tourist office	

Vocabulary   Everyday activities
Grammar   Adverbs of frequency
Language to go   Talking about how often you do things

Sports personality of the year

Aim

To practise *How often* and adverbs of frequency to talk about routines

Materials

One copy of the worksheet cut in half per pair

Time

30 minutes

Preparation

Photocopy the worksheet and cut it in half, one for Student A and one for Student B

Procedure

1 Brainstorm the names of sports and famous sports personalities on the board.
2 Divide the students into small groups of two or three. There must be an even number of groups in order to divide them into As and Bs.
3 Set the scene by telling Group A that they are a famous sports personality who is going to be interviewed by an English-speaking journalist. Before the interview, they are given the questions the interviewer may ask them to help them prepare for the interview. Group B are the journalists from a sports paper (use one the students may know as an example).
4 Give out part A of the worksheet to Student A and part B to Student B.
5 Tell Group A to decide what their name is and what sport they do and imagine answers to the question prompts, for example, for food: *They sometimes eat chicken but they never eat fish*. Students can invent or use real personalities. Tell Group B to prepare the questions they are going to ask. Go round and help with grammar and vocabulary as necessary.
6 Divide the class into pairs, one from Group A and one from B. Demonstrate the activity with a student before getting them to interview each other.
7 Hold class feedback where the journalist tells the class about their sports personality and why they are famous.

Extension

Students change over and A becomes the journalist and B the sports personality. Students write the article for homework or the class/school magazine.

Sheet A

Interview Questions for Press conference (16 Feb)

Diet (food and drink):
 What?
 How often?

Daily routines:
 What?
 How often?

Free time:
 What?
 How often?

Holidays:
 Where?
 How often?

Relationships:
 boy/girlfriend?
 How often/see her/him?

Sheet B

Relationships: boy/girlfriend? How often do you see her/him?

Daily routine: What? How often?

Holidays: How often? Where?

Free time: What? How often?

Diet (food and drink): What? How often?

Vocabulary Furniture in an office / living room
Grammar Prepositions of place
Language to go Telling someone where things are in a room

Interior design

Aim

To practise prepositions of place and furniture vocabulary

Materials

One copy of the rolecard for Student A and B
One copy of the cut-up furniture per student and a blank sheet of paper and a pen

Time

30 minutes

Preparation

Photocopy and cut up the rolecards. Photocopy and cut up the furniture cards.

Procedure

1 Draw a plan of a room on the board. The room **must** be square with the door in the middle of the bottom line and the window in the middle of the left hand line. Ask students to each make a large copy of this on a whole sheet of A4 paper.
2 Divide the students into pairs and set the scene. Write *interior design* on the board and check students know the meaning. Explain that Student B is an interior designer who thinks that the place you put your furniture can change your life and make you happy or rich or even unhappy. Tell Student A they live in a flat and they want to phone an interior design expert and check the position of the furniture in the room. Tell Student B they are an interior designer.
3 Give the students the rolecards and cut up furniture and tell them to put the furniture on the plan according to their rolecards. They must keep the plans secret from each other.
4 Tell Student A to ring Student B and describe the flat. Student B must tell Student A to move the furniture according to his/her interior design. Student A must listen to the advice and move the furniture on the plan.
5 Hold class feedback. Students reveal their plans to each other and check to see if they both have the furniture in the same place. Ask the class which layout they prefer: before or after the interior designer.

Extension

Students repeat the activity without the rolecards.
Students repeat the activity with a different plan. This could be more personalised, for example, students put the furniture in a plan of their classroom or school reception.

Student A	Student B
Describe your flat. You have the:	For good interior design you need the:
1 desk in front of the window	1 desk opposite the door
2 sofa opposite the desk	2 sofa in front of the window
3 cupboard opposite the door	3 cupboard next to the sofa and the door
4 computer on the desk	4 computer on the desk
5 calendar on the wall next to the window	5 calendar on the desk
6 lamp next to the sofa	6 lamp next to the sofa and the desk
7 bookcase next to the cupboard	7 bookcase opposite the sofa
8 plants next to the window under the calendar	8 plants on the cupboard
9 printer on the desk	9 printer under the desk
10 stereo on the cupboard	10 stereo on the bookcase
11 bin under the desk	11 bin under the desk
12 chair in front of the desk	12 chair in front of the desk

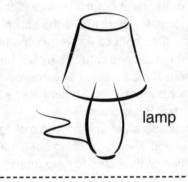
lamp

computer

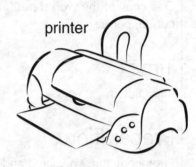
printer

calendar

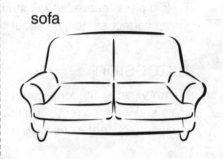
sofa

chair

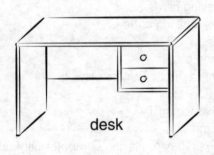
desk

plant

bookcase

stereo

bin

cupboard

Vocabulary Family
Grammar Present continuous for now
Language to go Talking about what your family / friends are doing

Sunday afternoon

Aim

To practise present continuous for actions happening now

Materials

One copy of the worksheet, cut up, per pair

Time

30 minutes

Preparation

Photocopy the worksheet and cut up the cards to give one set of cut up cards per pair.

Procedure

1 Brainstorm what activities people do on a rainy, Sunday afternoon, for example: play games, watch TV, read the newspaper, go for a walk.
2 Divide the students into pairs and give each pair a set of jumbled cut up cards.
3 Tell the students to put the cards face down in four rows of six.
4 Student A turns a card and makes a sentence about the picture in the present continuous. Then Student A turns another card. If the action (but not the person) doesn't match the first, both cards are returned face down and the game continues. If the second card is a match (the action but not the person), then Student A makes another sentence about the picture. If both sentences are correct, then Student A keeps the pair and wins one point. Then Student B has a turn.
5 Demonstrate the activity with the class and show them what makes a pair, for example, *He's drinking beer* and *They're drinking beer* is a pair. Tell them to remember the position of the cards to help them win more points.
6 Hold class feedback. Ask students to show you two cards and give you correct sentences about them.

Extension

Memory game. Students turn the cards over so they can't see them again and write correct sentences about the pictures. The pair with the most correct sentences wins.

ANSWER KEY

1 He's playing cards. She's playing cards.
2 They're drinking coffee. He's drinking coffee.
3 He's cooking. They're cooking.
4 He's eating pizza. She's eating pizza.
5 He's playing the guitar/an instrument. They're playing instruments.
6 She's watching TV. They're watching TV.
7 She's dancing. They're dancing.
8 He's playing computer games. They're playing computer games.
9 She's listening to music/a personal stereo. He's listening to music/a personal stereo.
10 She's reading a magazine. He's reading a magazine.
11 She's doing aerobics. They're doing aerobics.
12 It's sleeping. They're sleeping.

 © Pearson Education 2002

Vocabulary   food and drink
Function   Making requests
Language to go   Ordering food and drink in a café

Coffee please!

Aim

To practise the language for ordering in a café

Materials

One copy of the worksheet per student

Time

25 minutes

Preparation

Photocopy the worksheet.

Procedure

1 Brainstorm the names of food and drink you can buy in a café.
2 Set the scene by telling the students they are hungry and are going to order lunch in a café.
3 Divide the class into pairs and give each student the worksheet.
4 Tell students to choose a picture and write a café conversation ordering the food in the picture.
5 Walk around the class and check that students are doing different pictures and that they have not all chosen the same one.
   Tell students to change if they have all chosen the same one.
   Then walk around and help students with grammar and vocabulary.
6 Ask the students to practise saying their dialogues in pairs before presenting them to the whole class. Help the students with any pronunciation problems.
7 Tell each pair to roleplay their conversation in front of the class. The students need to listen and choose which picture from the worksheet corresponds to the conversation they can hear.

Extension

Students choose a new picture and repeat the activity. Tell the waiter and the customer to change roles so Student A and B have a chance to practise both sides of the conversation.

1  £10.25

2  £10.75

3  £11.25

4  £10.75

5  £10.25

6  £8.50

7  £5.50

8  £6.75

© *Pearson Education 2002*

Vocabulary   Activities at work
Grammar   *Can* for ability
Language to go   Asking about job skills

Perfect colleagues

Aim

To practise using *can* / *can't* for ability

Materials

One set of cards per 15 students

Time

20–30 minutes

Preparation

Photocopy and cut up enough cards for your class (see Procedure).

Procedure

1 Elicit / Check the verbs used in the activity by asking students what kind of things you may need to do if you work in an office / work with computers / work as an actor.
2 Explain that they will each have a card saying what they can do, and they must find two other people with the same abilities, i.e. 'perfect colleagues'. Demonstrate with two students. Give one of them a card that matches yours, and the second one a card that doesn't. Ask the second student the information on your card, for example, *Can you type? Can you dance?* Until you get the answer *No, I can't*. Then move on to the first student, who will answer *Yes, I can.* to all the questions. Tell the class that you have found one of your perfect colleagues, and you would now have to go round asking questions to find your second one.
3 Give out a card to each student. Each horizontal row forms a set of three. Make sure that complete sets of three of each card are given out. If your class is not an exact multiple of three, you will have to give out just two cards from one row. If you have more than fifteen students, it may be better for the class to work in two separate groups, with the right number of cards given to each group.
4 Students go round the class asking their questions. Monitor to make sure everyone is doing the activity correctly, and help with any language problems.
5 When everyone has found their perfect colleagues, hold quick feedback to find out what each group of perfect colleagues can do.

Extension

In the same groups, students could ask each other which of the activities on their cards they can really do.

ANSWER KEY
The horizontal rows of cards match:
A-H-O   G-B-K   F-C-L   N-D-I   E-J-M

A — You can …

type
write a computer programme
sing
speak a foreign language
play an instrument
dance

H — You can …

type
write a computer programme
sing
speak a foreign language
play an instrument
dance

O — You can …

type
write a computer programme
sing
speak a foreign language
play an instrument
dance

G — You can …

type
write a computer programme
sing
speak a foreign language
design a website
dance

B — You can …

type
write a computer programme
sing
speak a foreign language
design a website
dance

K — You can …

type
write a computer programme
sing
speak a foreign language
design a website
dance

F — You can …

type
dance
speak a foreign language
design a website
repair a computer
play an instrument

C — You can …

type
dance
speak a foreign language
design a website
repair a computer
play an instrument

L — You can …

type
dance
speak a foreign language
design a website
repair a computer
play an instrument

N — You can …

type
dance
design a website
repair a computer
play an instrument
speak a foreign language
write a computer programme

D — You can …

type
dance
design a website
repair a computer
play an instrument
speak a foreign language
write a computer programme

I — You can …

type
dance
design a website
repair a computer
play an instrument
speak a foreign language
write a computer programme

E — You can …

dance
sing
repair a photocopier
write a computer programme
design a website
speak a foreign language

J — You can …

dance
sing
repair a photocopier
write a computer programme
design a website
speak a foreign language

M — You can …

dance
sing
repair a photocopier
write a computer programme
design a website
speak a foreign language

Vocabulary Question words
Grammar Past simple of *be: was, were*
Language to go Talking about childhood memories

Liar liar!

Aim

Past simple/talking about one's past with *was/were*

Materials

One copy of the survey for each student

Time

30+ minutes

Preparation

The teacher should fill out the worksheet for him/herself ahead of time. Half the statements he/she writes are true and the other half are false.

Procedure

1 The survey contains ten questions about students' pasts. Before class, fill out the survey yourself. BUT, for half your answers, write lies.

2 Hand out one worksheet to each student. At this point, go through each question and read out your own response. This way, students will also get the structure. After you've finished, explain to the students that half the things you said were NOT true. Have them guess which things were lies.

3 Read through the instructions with the students. Make sure they know that half the answers they write should NOT be true. Give them a time limit to fill in their answers.

4 When students have finished writing, ask them to write their names on the worksheets. Collect the worksheets, shuffle and redistribute them, making sure nobody gets their own survey.

5 Explain that you are now going to see how well they know each other AND who the best liar is! Tell students to read through the surveys and decide whether the statements are true or false. They must circle T or F according to what they believe.

6 When they've finished, they can hand the survey back to the owner. For every statement that their partner has guessed correctly, they are given a point. The person with the fewest points is the winner, and the best liar in the class!

7 You may want to choose a few students and ask them one of the survey questions, then have the class, as a whole, decide if it's true or false – just for a bit of fun.

ANSWER KEY

Answers will vary, but make sure the written statements are in the correct form.

Liar, liar!

Survey

Answer the questions. Write true answers for five questions and false answers for five questions. Do not mark T or F yet!

1   How old was your first boyfriend or girlfriend?

_____   T   F

2   Where were you born?

_____   T   F

3   When were you born?

_____   T   F

4   Where was your best holiday?

_____   T   F

5   Who was your favourite singer when you were young?

_____   T   F

6   What was the first film you ever saw?

_____   T   F

7   When was your first driving lesson?

_____   T   F

8   Where were you for the millennium?

_____   T   F

9   Where were you last weekend?

_____   T   F

10   What was your first pet's name?

_____   T   F

My name _____

My points _____

Vocabulary Everyday activities
Grammar Past simple regular verbs (positive and negative)
Language to go Talking about your week

The singer and the star

Aim

Past tense (simple)

Materials

One complete reading and one gap-fill for each student

Time

20+ minutes

Preparation

Photocopy and cut up the cards.

Procedure

1 Separate students into pairs. Give one student card A1 and the other card A2. Have them look at the picture and read the short biography. This is about a fictional singer, Lyla Minuet.

2 Student A1 has a complete story about what Lyla did yesterday. Student A2 is missing some words. Tell Student A2 to ask questions to A1 to find out what Lyla did yesterday. You may want to write a few prompts on the board: *Who call … What wash … When finish …* to help students with what types of questions they will ask.

3 When Student A2 has filled in the gaps, hand out cards B1 and B2 and have students switch roles. Do the same exercise for the fictional movie star: Gary Garcia.

Extension

If you wish, ask students to write what Lyla or Gary do (usually) using the same verbs, but inserting the present simple as revision. Alternatively, students could write down what THEY did yesterday.

ANSWER KEY

Card A: mother, face, tennis, radio, 10 a.m., 8 p.m., boyfriend, music video

Card B: girlfriend, Mercedes Benz, music, 1 p.m., 11:30 p.m., girlfriend, news

A1

Lyla Minuet is a famous singer.
She is very busy. This is what Lyla
did yesterday:

Lyla called her mother. Then, she
washed her face. After that, she played
tennis and listened to the radio.
She started work at 10 a.m.
She finished work at 8 p.m. Then, she
danced with her boyfriend!
Finally, she watched a music video
on television.

A2

Lyla Minuet is a famous singer.
She is very busy. This is what Lyla
did yesterday:

Lyla called her _____ . Then, she
washed her _____ . After that,
she played _____ and listened to
the _____ .
She started work at _____ .
She finished work at _____ .
Then, she danced with her _____ !
Finally, she watched a _____
_____ on television.

B1

Gary Garcia is a famous movie star.
He is always busy. This is what he
did yesterday:

First, Gary called his girlfriend.
Then, he washed his Mercedes Benz.
After that he listened to some music.
He started work at 1 p.m.
He finished work at 11:30 p.m.
Then, he danced with his girlfriend!
Finally, he came home and watched
the news on television.

B2

Gary Garcia is a famous movie star.
He is always busy. This is what he
did yesterday:

First, Gary called his _____ .
Then, he washed his _____ _____ .
After that he listened to some _____ .
He started work at _____ .
He finished work at _____ .
Then, he danced with his _____ !
Finally, he came home and watched
the _____ on television.

Vocabulary Common irregular verbs
Grammar Past simple irregular verbs
Language to go Telling a story

Romeo and Juliet

Aim

Past tense irregular verbs, story-telling

Materials

One set of story cards for each pair of students

Time

20–25 minutes

Preparation

Cut apart the story cards, and write the following verbs on the board: *is/are, name, live, meet, think, go, see, tell, hate, fall, leave, find.*

Procedure

1 Ask students if they know any famous love stories. Tell them you are thinking of one particular famous couple and see if they can guess. When the topic *Romeo and Juliet* has been introduced, separate students into pairs and hand out one set of story cards to each pair.

2 Point to the verbs written on the board. Explain to the students that there are gaps on the cards and that they must choose a verb from the board. Ask students if they can use the verbs or if they have to change them (just to get them used to the idea that this story is finished time and therefore they have to use the past tense). You may want to quiz students, orally, on the past tense forms of the verbs. (Note: the verb *hate* is not in the lesson in the book. Make sure they know what it means and the past tense form.) Then tell students to fill in the gaps on the story cards.

3 When they've finished, explain that the story of *Romeo and Juliet* is on the cards, but that it is all mixed up. Ask students to read the cards and try to put the story in the correct order.

4 Check that the story is in order by choosing different students to read one card at a time.

Extension

Have them write a short love story of their own. Ask them to use the same verbs that were used in the book and the activity.

ANSWER KEY

Gapfill: Card one: named, lived, was
Card two: met, thought
Card three: went, saw, told
Card four: hated
Card five: went
Card six: went, fell, saw, left
Card seven: found, thought, saw, was

Many years ago, there was a boy _____ Romeo and a girl named Juliet. They _____ in Italy. Romeo was sixteen and Juliet _____ fourteen.

Romeo and Juliet _____ at a party at Juliet's house. Romeo _____ Juliet was very beautiful.

Romeo _____ to Juliet's window that night. He _____ her standing on a balcony. He _____ Juliet he loved her and she said she loved him too.

But, there was a problem. Juliet's family _____ Romeo's family, and Romeo's family hated Juliet's family!

The next day, Romeo and Juliet _____ to a church. They were married!

Juliet _____ home. She drank some poison and _____ asleep. Juliet's family _____ her and thought she was dead! They _____ her in a tomb.

When Romeo _____ Juliet, he _____ she was dead too. Romeo killed himself. When Juliet woke up, she _____ Romeo. She killed herself too. It _____ a sad story.

Vocabulary   Verbs and nouns: important events in life
Grammar   Past simple (questions)
Language to go   Asking questions to find out about people's lives

Who am I?

Aim

Past tense: *was*, *were*/asking questions with *who*, *what*, *where*, *when*, *how*

Materials

One question sheet for each student
One set of biography cards for each group

Time

20–30 minutes

Preparation

Cut up the biography cards. Copy enough question sheets for one for each student.

Procedure

1 On the board write: *Who am I?* Use one of the biography cards and read one fact at a time. After each fact, ask students 'Who am I?' Wait until they guess who you are. If they can't guess, tell them to ask you questions and give them answers until they know who you are.
The structure should be in the first person so that *was* and *were* forms are used.
2 Separate students into small groups. Hand out one question sheet to each student. Ask students to look at the question sheet. Make sure they know how to use the prompts to ask a question. Simply go through them with the class as a whole.
3 Hand out one completed biography card to each student. Tell them NOT to show their cards to their partners. Ask students to read through the biographical information.
4 When they have finished reading, students take turns asking and answering questions. They must try to figure out who their partner is. Tell students to use their question sheets to ask questions.
5 When everyone has figured out who their partner is, several students can introduce themselves (in first person), or introduce each other to the class.

Extension

Tell each student to write their own biography card. Mix them up.
Hand them out and ask students to read and guess who the biographies belong to.

Who am I?

Leonardo Da Vinci

I was born in Italy.
I lived in Milan.
I was an artist and inventor.
I wasn't married.
I was short and had a beard.
I died naturally.

Marilyn Monroe

I was born in the USA.
I lived in Hollywood.
I was an actress.
I married three different people.
I was blonde and beautiful!
I died when I was thirty-six.

Gandhi

I was born in India.
I lived in England and India.
I was a politician.
I got married.
I was small and had no hair.
Someone murdered me.

Cleopatra

I was born in Egypt.
I lived in Egypt and Rome.
I was a political leader.
I fell in love with Mark Anthony.
I was very beautiful.
I killed myself with a poisonous snake!

William Shakespeare

I was born in
  Stratford-upon-Avon.
I lived in London.
I was a writer and actor.
I married Anne Hathaway.
I was bald and had a beard.
I died when I was fifty-two.

Abraham Lincoln

I was born in the USA.
I lived in Washington DC.
I was a President.
I married Martha Lincoln.
I was very tall.
Someone shot me in a theatre!

Ask your partner ...

1 where ... born?
  'Where were you born?'
2 where ... live?
3 what ... job?
4 get ... married?
5 what ... look like?
6 how / when ... die?

Make a biography for you:

1 I was born in _____.

2 I lived _____.

3 _____.

4 _____.

5 _____.

6 _____.

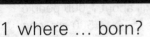

Vocabulary   Numbers
Grammar   Questions with *How* + adjective
Language to go   Asking for and giving measurements

Rivers

Aim

To practise questions with *how* + adjective (*how far, long, high, fast, heavy, deep*) and revise large numbers

Materials

One copy of the worksheet cut in half per student

Time

25 minutes

Preparation

Photocopy the worksheet and cut it in half.

Procedure

1 Set the scene. Play 'Hangman' with a river from the students' country or a river they all know. Then play 'Hangman' with the rivers Amazon and Zambezi. Ask students what they know about the Amazon and the Zambezi, for example, *Where they are? What animals are there? How long are they?*

2 Divide the students into pairs. Give Student A, part A of the worksheet and Student B, part B of the worksheet. Tell the students they have different information about the Amazon and the Zambezi and that they need to ask questions to complete the information they do not have. The first text has prompts to help the students form the correct questions. Use the prompts to demonstrate the activity with a student.

3 Check students can make the *how* + adjective questions and can use *cm*, *km/h* and *kgs*.

4 When students have finished asking and answering questions about the first text, demonstrate how to make questions without the prompts so that the students can complete the information on the second text.

5 Hold class feedback and elicit the answers for the questions.

ANSWERS

The Amazon river is 6,400 km long and goes from the Andes mountains to the Atlantic Ocean. Here, the river is 12 m deep, and 20% of the world's fresh water goes into the Atlantic Ocean every day. In the Amazon jungle you can find 1,100 different rivers, 16,600 different types of plants and 1,500 different types of fish and animals. For example, the anaconda weighs 148 kg and is up to 650 cm long. There is also the river dolphin. It's 250 cm long, can swim at 3 km/h, weighs 110 kg and lives in groups of 5–10. But it is difficult to see them because they are also very shy.

In the centre of Southern Africa is the Zambezi river or 'River of Life'. The source is 1,460 m high in the mountains of Angola and it is 2,700 km long. Each year crocodiles kill about 1,000 people in the rivers of Africa. An African crocodile is up to 500 cm long and weighs 850 kg and can run at 40 km/h for short distances. But don't worry about the crocodiles. Hippos are the most dangerous animals in Africa. They are up to 500 cm long, they weigh 3,500 kg, they can run at 45 km/h and they kill more people than any other African animal.

Sheet A

The Amazon river is 6,400 km long and goes from the Andes mountains to the Atlantic Ocean. Here, the river is (How deep?) _____ m deep, and 20% of the world's fresh water goes into the Atlantic Ocean every day. In the Amazon jungle you can find 1,100 different rivers, 16,600 different types of plants and 1,500 different types of fish and animals. For example, the anaconda weighs (How heavy?) _____ kg and is up to 650 cm long. There is also the river dolphin. It's (How long?) _____ cm long, can swim at 3 km/h, weighs (How heavy?) _____ and lives in groups of 5–10. But it's difficult to see them because they are also very shy.

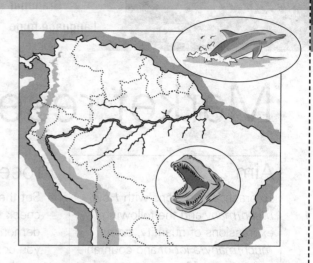

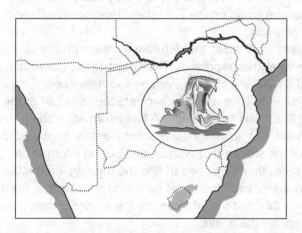

In the centre of Southern Africa is the Zambezi river or 'River of Life'. The source is 1,460 m high in the mountains of Angola and it is _____ km long. Each year, crocodiles kill about 1,000 people in the rivers of Africa. An African crocodile is up to 500 cm long and weighs _____ kg and can run at 40 km/h for short distances. But don't worry about the crocodiles. Hippos are the most dangerous animals in Africa. They are up to _____ cm long, they weigh 3,500 kg, they can run at _____ km/h and they kill more people than any other African animal.

Sheet B

The Amazon river is (How long?) _____ km long and goes from the Andes mountains to the Atlantic Ocean. Here, the river is 12 m deep, and 20% of the world's fresh water goes into the Atlantic Ocean every day. In the Amazon jungle you can find (How many?) _____ different rivers, 16,600 different types of plants and 1,500 different types of fish and animals. For example, the anaconda weighs 148 kg and is up to (How long?) _____ cm long. There is also the river dolphin. It's 250 cm long, can swim at (how fast) _____ km/h, weighs 110 kg and lives in groups of 5–10. But it's difficult to see them because they are also very shy.

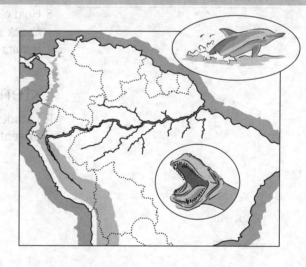

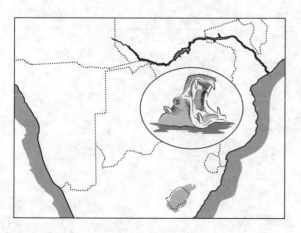

In the centre of Southern Africa is the Zambezi river or 'River of Life'. The source is _____ m high in the mountains of Angola and it is 2,700 km long. Each year, crocodiles kill about 1,000 people in the rivers of Africa. An African crocodile is up to _____ cm long and weighs 850 kg and can run at _____ km/h for short distances. But don't worry about the crocodiles. Hippos are the most dangerous animals in Africa. They are up to 500 cm long, they weigh _____ kg, they can run at 45 km/h and they kill more people than any other African animal.

Vocabulary Countable and uncountable nouns
Grammar Expressions of quantity
Language to go Talking about food you like

Market research

Aim

To practise questions with *How much/many* and the following expressions of quantity: *some/ much/many/a lot of* and countable and uncountable nouns

Materials

One copy of the worksheet cut in half per pair

Time

25 minutes

Preparation

Photocopy and cut up the worksheet.

Procedure

1 Set the scene by showing the students the graph. Make sure you check the meaning of *market research* and *snacks*. You could demonstrate *market research* by doing a quick class poll. For example, you could ask each student how many hours they study English a week. Explain that the graph on the worksheet represents different snacks which people eat.

2 Explain the graph by pointing to the different symbols on the vertical axis and eliciting what they represent. Then point to the horizontal axis and check the meaning of *light*, *average* and *heavy user*.

3 Divide the students into pairs and give each student one half of the worksheet, A or B. Explain that Student A has information about the snacks that men eat, but no information about women. Student B has information about the snacks that women eat, but no information about men. Tell them that they need to find the missing information on men and women for each food type by asking their partner for the information. When they get the information, the students then draw the correct size bar on the graph.

4 Demonstrate the activity with one student before letting the students finish the activity.

5 Hold class feedback. Tell the students to compare their graphs and check they have the correct size bars. Discuss as a class whether the results on the graphs are similar to the class as a whole.

Extension

Tell students to interview the other students and produce a graph that represents the whole class.

Sheet A

UK Market Research

Consumption of snacks
(men and women aged 25–45)

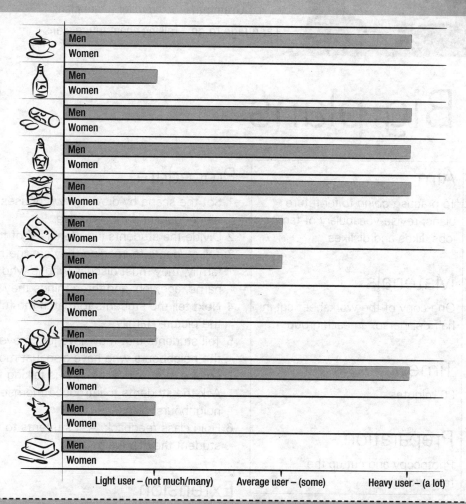

Light user – (not much/many)   Average user – (some)   Heavy user – (a lot)

Sheet B

UK Market Research

Consumption of snacks
(men and women aged 25–45)

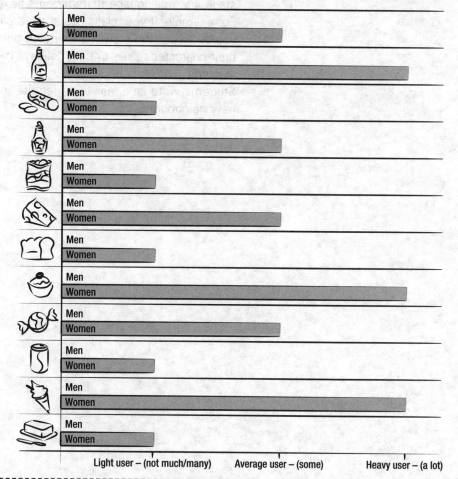

Light user – (not much/many)   Average user – (some)   Heavy user – (a lot)

Vocabulary Verbs and nouns describing changes in life
Grammar *Going to* for future plans
Language to go Talking about future plans

Big plans

Aim

To practise *going to* for future plans; revise vocabulary of family, jobs, likes and dislikes

Materials

One copy of the worksheet cut in half per person in each group

Time

30 minutes

Preparation

Photocopy and cut up the rolecards.

Procedure

1 Set the scene by drawing two houses on the board and pre-teach *neighbours* and *move house*.
2 Divide the students into 'families' of four. Give students the rolecards.
3 Tell students to imagine they are the family on the rolecard. As a family, they must discuss who is who and decide on each member's name, age, job, and three things they like.
4 Next tell the students to match the future plans to the individuals in the picture / family.
5 Tell students that they have just moved house and are going to meet the neighbours who have also just moved in. Rearrange the groups so one member of family A is talking to a member of family B.
Ask the students to introduce themselves and find out about their neighbours' plans.
6 Hold class feedback. Ask students to tell you about the plans of the student they spoke to.

Extension

You can make this into a revision activity by replacing the prompts in stage 4 with language that students have covered recently in class. For example, if your class has studied *can* for ability, or the past simple, you could ask the students to invent personalised information about their character's skills or past holidays based on the language to be revised.
Students write an e-mail to a friend telling them about their new neighbours.

Sheet A

go to university / school

get a part time job

have a baby

build a new kitchen

give up smoking

change job

earn a lot of money

do the gardening

lose weight

leave boy/girlfriend

?

?

learn to play an instrument

buy a pet

get married

Sheet B

go to university / school

get a part time job

have a baby

build a new kitchen

give up smoking

change job

earn a lot of money

do the gardening

lose weight

leave boy/girlfriend

?

?

learn to play an instrument

buy a pet

get married

Vocabulary   Parts of a public building; American English
Grammar   Prepositions of movement
Language to go   Asking and giving directions

Directions

Aim

To practise giving directions inside a building

Materials

1 copy of Plan A and B per student and 1 set of directions per student

Time

30 minutes

Preparation

Photocopy the worksheet. Separate the plans from the directions. One student will need Plan A, Plan B and one set of directions.

Procedure

1 The overall aim of this two-stage problem-solving activity is for the students in their own group to complete their plan of a leisure and entertainment complex, then communicate this information to students in the other group.
2 Divide the students into an even number of small groups of three or four students. Give A and B groups their respective plans and directions.
3 Explain that the students need to read the directions and write the names of the places on the plan.
4 Students read the information and write the names of the five places.
5 Check that each group has the correct order written down.
6 Reorganise the students into pairs, one from each group and give each student a new plan (but no directions). Student A should have Plan B and Student B should have Plan A.
7 Explain that the students now need to say the directions so that their partner can find the places on their new plan.

Extension

Tell students to choose different places on the plan and ask for and give directions in pairs. Students can write directions for a guest, from the lift to room 101.

ANSWER KEY
A 1 Palace theatre   3 Olympics gym   8 Odeon cinema
11 Piccadilly bar   7 Tower restaurant   6 Room 101
B 1 Maxi cinema   6 Park gym   5 Palace restaurant
8 Regency bar   7 ADC theatre   9 Room 101

Sheet A

Directions A

1 Come out of the lift and you'll see the Palace Theatre on the right.
2 Go past the theatre and turn left.
3 Go along the corridor and you'll see the Olympics gym on the left. It's opposite the theatre.
4 Turn right after the gym and you'll see the Odeon cinema on the left.
5 Turn left after the cinema. The Piccadilly bar is on the right, opposite the cinema.
6 Turn left and go along the corridor. You'll see the Tower restaurant on the right.
7 Go past the Tower restaurant and Room 101 is in front of you.

Plan A

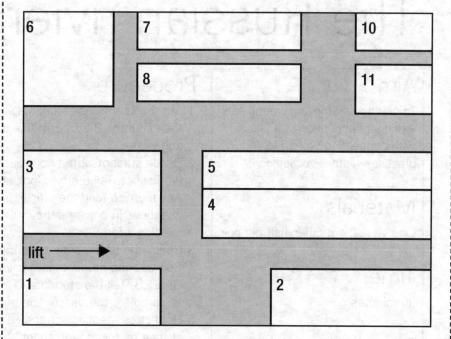

Sheet B

Directions B

1 Come out of the lift and you'll see the Maxi cinema on the right.
2 Go past the cinema and turn left.
3 Go along the corridor and you'll see the Park gym in front of you.
4 Turn left and then turn right. The Palace restaurant is on the left. It's opposite the gym.
5 Turn right and go past the gym. The Regency bar is on the left. It's opposite the gym.
6 Go along the corridor. The ADC theatre is on the right. It's next to the gym.
7 Turn left and Room 101 is on the right.

Plan B

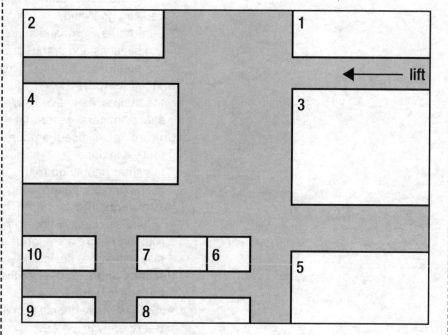

 © Pearson Education 2002

Vocabulary **Weather**
Grammar **Linking words:** *because, so, but, although*
Language to go **Describing climate and lifestyle**

The Russian riviera

Aim

To practise asking/answering and writing a description of a place with connecting words; to practise weather vocabulary

Materials

One worksheet cut in half per pair

Time

30 minutes

Preparation

Photocopy the worksheet and cut it in half.

Procedure

1 Set the scene. Ask students where the best holiday towns are in their country. Brainstorm things you can do in these towns in summer and winter.
2 Divide students into two groups, As and Bs. Give students the worksheet. Tell them to look at the pictures and tell you about Sochi. Ask them to read the article. In groups, the students prepare the questions in brackets they want to ask in order to find out the missing information.
3 Check the two groups have the correct questions.
4 Regroup the students into pairs, one from Group A and one from Group B. Tell the students to ask questions and write the information to complete the description of Sochi.
5 Hold class feedback on the correct answers. Tell students to look at their partner's worksheet.

Extension

Students write a website for a place they know well in their country using the same categories as for Sochi.

ANSWERS

Weather In winter it is warm because it is next to the sea.
There are also mountains near Sochi, so from October to May you can go skiing.
Summer is warm and sunny so there are a lot of tropical plants like bananas and orange trees. Although it is windy, the temperature is nice so many people come for a holiday.

Special features Stalin had a house here but it is not open to the public. Many old people also come because Sochi has special mineral water that people drink all over Russia.

Culture You can see famous movie stars because there is a film festival in June.
In winter people go to the Winter Theatre but in summer there is an open-air theatre.

Restaurants and nightlife There are many open-air restaurants so you can always find something good to eat.
Although there are a lot of nightclubs, they are expensive and play the same music.

Beaches Although the beaches are black, they are beautiful and the sea is warm.

Activities Many people visit in May because there is the 'Sea of Beer' festival.
Although the skiing is good, you can also go mountain climbing or have a Russian 'vanya' or sauna.

Sheet A

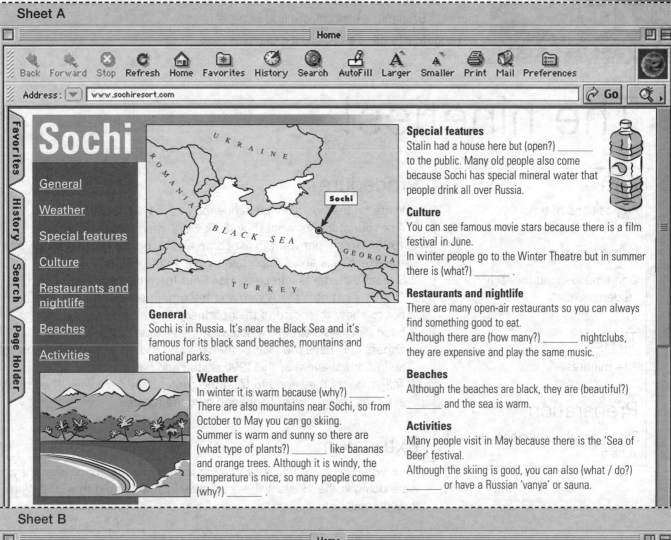

Sochi

www.sochiresort.com

- General
- Weather
- Special features
- Culture
- Restaurants and nightlife
- Beaches
- Activities

General
Sochi is in Russia. It's near the Black Sea and it's famous for its black sand beaches, mountains and national parks.

Weather
In winter it is warm because (why?) _____ . There are also mountains near Sochi, so from October to May you can go skiing. Summer is warm and sunny so there are (what type of plants?) _____ like bananas and orange trees. Although it is windy, the temperature is nice, so many people come (why?) _____ .

Special features
Stalin had a house here but (open?) _____ to the public. Many old people also come because Sochi has special mineral water that people drink all over Russia.

Culture
You can see famous movie stars because there is a film festival in June.
In winter people go to the Winter Theatre but in summer there is (what?) _____ .

Restaurants and nightlife
There are many open-air restaurants so you can always find something good to eat.
Although there are (how many?) _____ nightclubs, they are expensive and play the same music.

Beaches
Although the beaches are black, they are (beautiful?) _____ and the sea is warm.

Activities
Many people visit in May because there is the 'Sea of Beer' festival.
Although the skiing is good, you can also (what / do?) _____ or have a Russian 'vanya' or sauna.

Sheet B

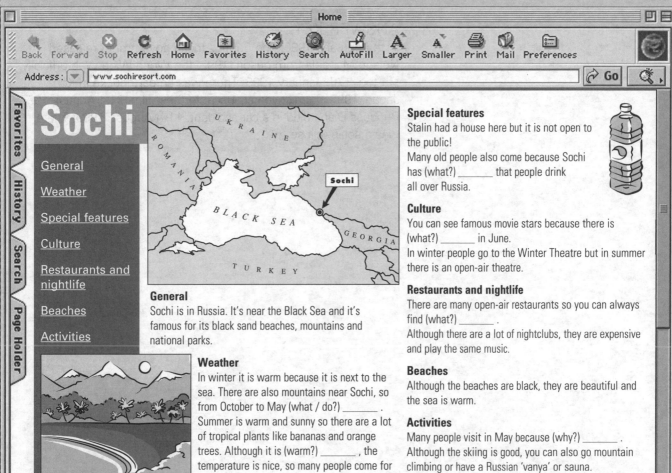

Sochi

www.sochiresort.com

- General
- Weather
- Special features
- Culture
- Restaurants and nightlife
- Beaches
- Activities

General
Sochi is in Russia. It's near the Black Sea and it's famous for its black sand beaches, mountains and national parks.

Weather
In winter it is warm because it is next to the sea. There are also mountains near Sochi, so from October to May (what / do?) _____ . Summer is warm and sunny so there are a lot of tropical plants like bananas and orange trees. Although it is (warm?) _____ , the temperature is nice, so many people come for a holiday.

Special features
Stalin had a house here but it is not open to the public!
Many old people also come because Sochi has (what?) _____ that people drink all over Russia.

Culture
You can see famous movie stars because there is (what?) _____ in June.
In winter people go to the Winter Theatre but in summer there is an open-air theatre.

Restaurants and nightlife
There are many open-air restaurants so you can always find (what?) _____ .
Although there are a lot of nightclubs, they are expensive and play the same music.

Beaches
Although the beaches are black, they are beautiful and the sea is warm.

Activities
Many people visit in May because (why?) _____ .
Although the skiing is good, you can also go mountain climbing or have a Russian 'vanya' or sauna.

Vocabulary Dates
Grammar Time prepositions: *in*, *on*, *at*
Language to go Talking about memorable times

The nineties!

Aim

Prepositions of time

Materials

One timeline card for each student

Time

20+ minutes

Preparation

Photocopy the worksheet and cut in half.

Procedure

1 Write on the board: *What happened in … What happened on …*
Ask your students what they think were important events in the 1990s. You might want to list some events on the board. Explain that the exercise is about important events in the 1990s.
2 Separate students into pairs. Hand out the timeline cards.
One student gets the A card and the other gets the B card. Tell them not to show their card to their partner.
3 Each card has a list of six dates. Some include a date and year. Others only have the year or the year and month. Half the cards have an important event of the 1990s listed and half are blank.
4 Tell students they need to fill in the gaps on their timeline. They must ask their partner what happened on certain dates.

Extension

For a writing activity, you may want students to write about what they were doing in the 1990s. Where did they live? What did they do? Were they married? etc. …

ANSWER KEY
11th February, 1990: The South African government released Nelson Mandela from prison. 1992: the World Wide Web officially started. 17th January 1995: There was an earthquake in Kobe, Japan. 1997: *Titanic* won an Oscar for best film. 31st August, 1997: Princess Diana died in a car accident. 11th August, 1999: There was a solar eclipse.

Sheet A

South Africa
released
Nelson Mandela
from prison

There was an
earthquake in
Kobe, Japan

Princess Diana
died in a
car accident

1992   1997   11th August
1999

11th February
1990   17th January
1995   31st August
1997

_____   _____   _____
_____   _____   _____
_____   _____   _____
_____   _____   _____

Sheet B

The World Wide
Web officially
started

Titanic won
an Oscar
for best film

There was a
solar eclipse

11th February
1990   17th January
1995   31st August
1997

1992   1997   11th August
1999

_____   _____   _____
_____   _____   _____
_____   _____   _____
_____   _____   _____

Vocabulary Everyday requests
Function Permission and requests
Language to go Asking for things and giving a response

Pearl and Naomi

Aim

Polite requests, refusals, etc.

Materials

Copies of the worksheet for each student

Time

25+ minutes

Preparation

Photocopy the worksheet.

Procedure

1 Write two words on the board: *polite* and *rude*. Give students some examples of being polite and being rude. Ask students what is considered polite/rude in their culture. Examples: *Is it rude to wear shoes in someone's house? Is it polite to bring a bottle of wine when you visit a friend's house?*

2 Hand out the worksheets (one per student). At the top of the page is a picture of two older women at tea. Pearl is obviously very well-mannered. Naomi is obviously rude. Ask students who they think is rude and who they think is polite. Ask them to explain why: *Naomi has put too much jam on her bread!* etc.

3 Below the picture is a list of eight different situations. Use the first situation as an example and ask students how they think the two women would respond in the situation. The idea is to get a rude response from Naomi and a polite response from Pearl.

4 Separate students into small groups. For each situation, the group must come up with a short written response of how the two women react in the given situations. For example: Naomi and Pearl are at a restaurant. They need some salt.
Pearl: Could I have some salt, please?
Naomi: Give me some salt!

5 When students have finished, use a few situations for a roleplay. Cast students as Naomi, Pearl and the waiter/clerk/stranger/bus driver. You can do this as a class, or in small groups.

Extension

You may want to ask students to write up a list of common requests, then practise, with a partner, giving polite responses.

ANSWER KEY
Answers will vary.

Sheet A

This is Naomi and Pearl.
Pearl is always polite.
Naomi is quite rude.
Look at the following situations.
What would Pearl say?
What would Naomi say?
Discuss it with your partner and
write your answers.

Naomi and Pearl are at a restaurant. They need some salt.

Naomi: _____

Pearl: _____

Naomi and Pearl are on the telephone. They can't hear each other.

Naomi: _____

Pearl: _____

The ladies are at tea. They want to offer a biscuit to their friend.

Naomi: _____

Pearl: _____

Naomi and Pearl need to borrow some money for their bus ticket.

Naomi: _____

Pearl: _____

The ladies want to pay for their shopping with a credit card.

Naomi: _____

Pearl: _____

Naomi and Pearl are on a bus. They want to ask the driver how to get to Ash Street.

Naomi: _____

Pearl: _____

The ladies are in a shoe shop. They want some black sandals.

Naomi: _____

Pearl: _____

Naomi and Pearl are in the street. They want to know the time.

Naomi: _____

Pearl: _____

Vocabulary Adjectives to describe places
Grammar Comparatives
Language to go Comparing places in your country

A tale of two cities

Aim

Adjectives to describe a location; comparatives, talking about cities

Materials

One copy of each half of the worksheet per student

Time

30+ minutes

Preparation

Photocopy the worksheet and cut it up. Possibly write the adjective list on board.

Procedure

1 First, ask students to describe the city you are in, maybe write what they tell you on the board. Review words used in the lesson (you may want to write them on the board as well):
historic cosmopolitan dirty/clean crowded beautiful modern quiet/noisy exciting/fun, etc.

2 Separate students into pairs and hand out the Rome card to one student and the Vancouver card to the other. Each card contains a short description of the city. Give them a few minutes to read through, then ask a few comprehension questions, such as: *What is the population of Vancouver? What are the industries of Rome?*

3 Hand out the second half of the worksheet. Point out the first adjective: *old.* Ask one student 'When was Vancouver built?' Then ask another 'When was Rome built?' Finally, give students the structure by saying, 'Aaah, Rome is OLDER than Vancouver.' Write this short dialogue on the board, so that students can see how the activity will be structured.

4 Students work in pairs and go through the other adjectives, by asking each other questions about the cities. Tell them to write down comparative sentences.

Extension

You may want to assign a short writing exercise. Ask students which city they would prefer living in. Ask them to write about their choice and why: *I want to live in Rome because it is warmer than Vancouver.*

ANSWER KEY
Answers may vary, but the basic idea is the following:
 1 Rome is older than Vancouver.
 2 Vancouver is newer than Rome.
 3 Rome is more crowded than Vancouver.
 4 Vancouver is emptier than Rome.
 5 Rome is warmer than Vancouver.
 6 Vancouver is cooler than Rome.
 7 Rome is more historic than Vancouver.
 8 Vancouver is more modern than Rome.
 9 Rome is flatter than Vancouver.
10 Vancouver is greener than Rome.
11 Vancouver is wetter than Rome.
12 Rome is drier than Vancouver.

Rome, Italy
built: 8 BC
population: three million people
industry: tourism, finance
climate: cool winter, hot and humid summers
countryside: hills, lakes
food / drink: pasta, pizza, wine
people: Italian, immigrants
famous for: fashion, food, history

Vancouver, Canada
built: early 1800s
population: two million people
industry: shipping, fishing, forest industry, tourism
climate: rainy, cold winters, warm summers
countryside: rain forest, mountains, seaside
food / drink: salmon, fish, fruit, beer
people: European and Asian
famous for: parks, natural beauty, animal life

Ask your partner about his / her city.
Compare them.
Which city is older?
Which city is newer?
Write one answer for each of the following adjectives.

1 old _____

2 new _____

3 crowded _____

4 empty _____

5 hot / warm _____

6 cold / cool _____

7 historic _____

8 modern _____

9 flat _____

10 green _____

11 wet _____

12 dry _____

 © Pearson Education 2002

Vocabulary Adjectives to describe restaurants
Grammar Superlatives
Language to go Describing restaurants

Best kept secrets

Aim

To practise superlative adjectives and to talk about places in a town / area

Materials

One copy of the worksheet per group
Counters for students

Time

30 minutes

Preparation

Photocopy the worksheet.

Procedure

1 Divide the students into groups of three or four and give each group the worksheet.
2 Explain that students are going to play a game in which they describe restaurants and cafés they know. Students throw a coin and move their counter forward (heads = 1 space and tails = 2 spaces). When students land on a square they must make a sentence about a place they know using an adjective in its superlative form and a restaurant or café they know, for example, *Arzak has the most delicious food* or *Amabost is the busiest bar*. If students land on a 'move' square, they must do what it says. Explain that this is a free speaking game and students can say as much or as little as they want. The winner is the first student to move their counter from the start to the finish.
4 Elicit some adjectives to describe cafés and restaurants. Write some adjectives on the board, for example: *romantic, busy, clean, delicious, friendly, good, famous, popular, comfortable* etc.
Then elicit some negative adjectives, such as: *unromantic, dirty, unfriendly* etc. Leave the adjectives on the board for students to refer to while they play the game.
5 Students start to play the game. Each student puts a counter on the Start / Finish square and takes it in turns to move around the board.
6 Have a class feedback session. Ask students what the others in their group answered on the different squares.

Extension

Students write their own board game on a different category, for example, best and worst shops or sports.

START ▷▷▷

Café

Move forward 1 square

Menu

Restaurant

Waiter / waitress

Food

Bar

Move back 1 square

Fast food place

Move back 1 square

Foreign restaurant

Drink

Service

FINISH ◁◁◁

Atmosphere

Move forward 1 square

Smooth operator

Aim

Practise using the telephone, taking and leaving messages

Materials

One set of rolecards for each group and one set of message templates

Time

25+ minutes

Preparation

Photocopy and cut up the cards.

Procedure

1 Separate students into pairs. Pass out the first set of cards (ie. two message templates and the contact cards for Mr Fujikawa (card A) and Ms Malone (card B)).
Each student needs to have a rolecard and a message template.

2 This is a telephone/message roleplay. Students will take turns being a secretary and being the caller. The caller uses their rolecard to make a call. They have the name of the person they want to contact and a short message to leave with the secretary.
The secretary has the message template. This student must ask the caller enough questions so that they can fill in the template. Also, they will need to write in the date and the time the call was made.

3 You may want to write a few prompts on the board: *May I leave a message? Would you like to leave a message? What is your number? When will he/she be back? Could you tell him/her …
I'm sorry, he/she's not in … How do you spell that?*

4 Begin the roleplay with Card A. Make sure that students know that the person being called is NOT in, and that they will be speaking to the secretary. Have Mr Fujikawa call Ms Malone's office and leave a message.

5 Students now swap roles. Ms Malone calls Mr Fujikawa's office and leaves a message for him. When the calls are finished and messages have been written, students can check how accurately they took messages by comparing their template with their partner's contact cards.

6 When the first roleplay is done, you may want to ask students to switch partners. Hand out the next set of four cards and tell them to repeat the same steps for these cards as well.

Extension

You can extend the roleplay by asking the secretary to call their boss and relay the message they've taken.

ANSWER KEY
Answers will vary.

Message   date: _____
time: _____

for: _____

caller: _____

telephone/fax number: _____

message: _____

_____

_____

_____

_____

Message   date: _____
time: _____

for: _____

caller: _____

telephone/fax number: _____

message: _____

_____

_____

_____

_____

Message   date: _____
time: _____

for: _____

caller: _____

telephone/fax number: _____

message: _____

_____

_____

_____

_____

Message   date: _____
time: _____

for: _____

caller: _____

telephone/fax number: _____

message: _____

_____

_____

_____

_____

Card A Mr Fujikawa

You are Mr Fujikawa. You want to speak to Ms Malone. You want to have lunch with her tomorrow at 12:30. Leave a message for her to call you back. Your telephone number is: 555 1213.

Card B Ms Malone

You are Ms Malone. You want to speak to Mr Fujikawa. You cannot meet him for lunch tomorrow at 12:30. You want to meet him at 1:30. Leave a message for him to call you back. Your telephone number is: 555 1312.

Card C Mr Black

You are Mr Black. You want to speak to Mr Grey. You want to know if he received your fax. Leave him a message to call you back. Your telephone number is 555 1992. Your fax number is 555 1994.

Card D Mr Grey

You are Mr Grey. You want to speak to Mr Black. Leave a message for him to send the fax again. You did not receive the fax. Ask him to call you when he sends the fax. Your telephone number is 555 2218. Your fax number is 555 2219.

Vocabulary Social etiquette
Grammar *Should* for advice
Language to go Giving advice to visitors

I need help!

Aim

Offering advice or suggestions

Materials

One or two cards for each student

Time

20–30 minutes

Preparation

Photocopy the cards. Cut up and fill in one yourself as an example.

Procedure

1 On the board, write out the following problem: *I am very shy. I have no friends and I am lonely. What should I do?* Have a short in-class discussion. Students can offer suggestions or advice.
2 Hand out one card to each student. Explain that the top portion of the card contains a problem. Explain that the bottom contains some advice or a suggestion. Point out that their suggestion and problem do not match. Tell them that another person in class has the proper suggestion / advice for their problem.
3 This is a mingling exercise. All students must stand up and mingle. You may want to do an example of what you're looking for conversation wise, with one of the students, for example:
What's your problem? I am shy and have no friends.
Oh. My card says you should cut your hair. That's not right.
Try to get across the idea that they have to find a suggestion that makes sense for their problem.
4 When they find someone who has the proper advice, that person tears off the bottom portion of their card and gives it to them.
5 The activity is finished when all students have advice for their problem. Check to see that students have the correct matches by asking what their problem is and what they should do.
If you have an odd number of students, you will need to take part in the activity yourself. Cards are numbered in the following way: 1/2, 2/1, which means card 1 has the advice for card 2 and card 2 has the advice for card 1, and so on. This activity can be for up to twelve students. If you have more than that, just make duplicate sets.

Extension

Ask students if they agree with the advice they've been given. Can they think of a better suggestion? What would they suggest?

ANSWER KEY
Card 1/2 matches 2/1; card 3/4 matches 4/3, etc.

I need help!

1/2

Problem: My mother-in-law never leaves my house!

Advice: You should move to the country where you haven't got many neighbours.

2/1

Problem: My neighbours are very noisy!

Advice: You should move to a different city, far away from her!

3/4

Problem: I am going to visit my friends in Japan. What gift should I take?

Advice: You should follow him, or get a detective to follow him!

4/3

Problem: My boyfriend stays out late every night, and never tells me where he was.

Advice: You should take them a bottle of wine or whisky.

5/6

Problem: My house is very small and I don't have much money.

Advice: You should wear something conservative and give them something to use in their new house.

6/5

Problem: I am going to an Indian wedding. What should I wear and what gift should I take?

Advice: You should put a lot of mirrors on your walls so it looks bigger.

7/8

Problem: My friend always borrows money from me and never returns it!

Advice: You should look for a new job.

8/7

Problem: My boss is always angry with me for no reason!

Advice: You should 'borrow' his car and 'forget' to return it until your friend returns your money!

9/10

Problem: My girlfriend wants to buy a dog but I hate dogs!

Advice: You should buy the cat and find a new boyfriend.

10/9

Problem: I want to buy a cat but my boyfriend hates cats!

Advice: You should buy a cat for her.

11/12

Problem: I have a job interview in English but I don't speak English very well.

Advice: You should go on a diet and try to stop smoking.

12/11

Problem: My doctor says I am too heavy and smoke too much.

Advice: You should take some English lessons.

© *Pearson Education 2002*

The wedding planner

Aim

Making suggestions, talking about money (a budget)

Materials

One copy of the worksheet for each small group

Time

25+ minutes

Preparation

Photocopy the worksheet.

Procedure

1 Introduce the topic by asking students what expenses there are when people get married. Elicit such responses as renting a church/hall/hotel, food, invitations, clothes, flowers, honeymoon.
2 Pass round the worksheet and have students read through the description of Mike and Georgia. Emphasise that Mike and Georgia have a specific budget. Also, ask a few comprehension questions such as *How much money have they got? What kind of wedding does Georgia want?*
3 Separate students into small groups or pairs. Tell them to read through the next section. Explain that they must plan Mike and Georgia's wedding. For each expense they have options. Students make suggestions to each other as to what they should choose.
4 You might want to write several prompts on the board: *We should … Let's … How about … I think …* to help with the discussion. Students should choose which option they feel best suits Mike and Georgia's wants, and stays within the budget.

Extension

Students can make a presentation of their ideas and suggestions back to the class, again using suggestion phrases.

ANSWER KEY
Answers will vary.

The wedding planner...

This is Mike and Georgia. They want to get married! Georgia wants a romantic wedding. Mike wants a small and simple wedding. Georgia loves flowers but Mike wants to have a nice honeymoon. Mike and Georgia don't have much money. They can only spend £3,000 on their wedding. Help them plan their wedding. Remember, don't spend too much money!

Discuss with your partner(s) then circle your choices.

wedding ceremony

church	£200
hall	£150
court	£50

wedding dress

Versace	£1,000
silk	£800
mother's dress	free!

reception

hotel	£1,500
restaurant	£1,000
pub	£500

flowers

roses	£400
carnations	£300
daisies	£200

invitations

expensive (gold ink)	£300
average price (silver ink)	£200
cheap (normal ink)	£150

honeymoon

Scotland	£500
Italy	£1,000
Tahiti	£2,000

Vocabulary   Movies
Grammar   *Say* and *tell*
Language to go   Talking about movies

The all-time Oscars!

Aim

Talking about movies, actors, favourites/superlatives: best and worst

Materials

One copy of the 'nominations' worksheet for each student. (Cut each worksheet in half. Each half is the same.)

Time

30+ minutes

Preparation

Photocopy the worksheet. Also, you may want to come up with a short list of local films, actors/actresses just in case your class has trouble thinking of any.

Procedure

1 To introduce the topic, ask questions such as: *What's your favourite movie?* or *Who's your favourite actor/actress?* You might even tell the class what/who your favourites are.

2 On the board write the word *Oscar*. Ask your class who *Oscar* is. Hand out the worksheets. Point to the picture of *Oscar*. Explain to the class that *Oscar* is an Academy Award.

3 The first part of the worksheet contains six categories for students to make nominations: *Best film of all time, Worst film of all time, Best actor of all time, Worst actor of all time, Best actress of all time, Worst actress of all time.* Ask students to write a nomination in each given space. Make sure they know that they can choose ANY film/actor (ALL TIME). If students are having trouble thinking of films or actors, give them a suggestion.

4 When students have finished writing their nominations, separate them into groups of three or four. They can start asking each other questions:
What is the best film of all time? Star Wars!
Why do you think it's the best? Because it has good special effects.
Who is the worst actress of all time? Demi Moore.
Why do you think that? Because I saw 'Striptease' and she was terrible!
You may want to write a sample dialogue on the board.

5 Give students enough time to have a good discussion. After they've talked about their choices, ask them to come up with a list of Oscar winners/losers within their groups. At this point, try to get them to start using *he said/ she said/ we said* (reported speech).

6 When each group has a list, they can report their award choice back to the class and see how their votes compare with others. At the end, you may want to add up all the votes and see who the winners are, according to the class.

Extension

You may want to do the same activity again, this time for music:
What's the best/ worst album of all time? Who's the best/ worst singer of all time?

ANSWER KEY
Answers will vary.

Sheet A

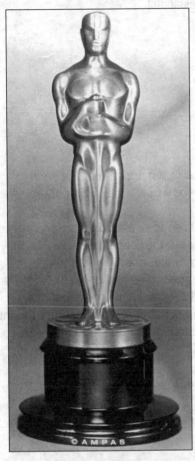

All-time Oscars! ★★★

Write the name of a film, actor or actress for each of the following categories:

1 Best film of all time:

_____

2 Worst film of all time:

_____

3 Best actor of all time:

_____

4 Worst actor of all time:

_____

5 Best actress of all time:

_____

6 Worst actress of all time:

_____

Sheet B

All-time Oscars! ★★★

Write the name of a film, actor or actress for each of the following categories:

1 Best film of all time:

_____

2 Worst film of all time:

_____

3 Best actor of all time:

_____

4 Worst actor of all time:

_____

5 Best actress of all time:

_____

6 Worst actress of all time:

_____

Vocabulary   Restaurant words
Grammar   *Would like/like, would prefer/prefer*
Language to go   Ordering food and drink in a restaurant

Fine dining

Aim

Eating at a restaurant
I like …
I would like …
I prefer …
I don't like …

Materials

Copies of the rolecards (one for each student) and one copy of the menu per group

Time

25+ minutes

Preparation

Copy the worksheet and cut up the rolecards. Copy one menu per group.

Procedure

1 Ask several students what they like to eat and drink. Use such phrases as *Do you prefer red wine or white wine? What do you like better, chicken or fish?*

2 Separate students into groups of three to five students. Hand out the rolecards (one per student). Make sure the students know that they are going to roleplay these characters (i.e. use first person).
Each character has a list of preferences, likes and dislikes. Give them a minute to read through their cards and ask you any questions.

3 Hand out one copy of the menu to each group. Appoint one student, in each group, to be the waiter/waitress. Use one student as an example to show what type of dialogue they are going to have in the roleplay:
Good evening. Are you ready to order?
Yes.
Would you like something to drink?
Yes, please. I'd like some wine.
Would you prefer red or white?
Red, please …
Again, you may want to write some prompts or a sample dialogue on the board. This is a basic restaurant roleplay with the exception that students must order according to the preferences on their rolecards.

4 Students take turns being the waiter/waitress in their groups.
To avoid repetition, tell them to exchange character cards as well.

Extension

You may wish to continue the roleplay based on the personal likes/dislikes/preferences of each student. Alternatively ask students what they would order from the menu, if they were visiting the restaurant.

ANSWER KEY
Answers will vary.

Mr Rao

He doesn't eat meat.

He likes vegetables, rice and pasta.

He prefers red wine.

He likes tea.

Ms Louis

She likes fish and seafood.

She doesn't like red meat.

She likes sweets.

She doesn't drink alcohol.

Mrs Gold

She likes soups and salads.

She doesn't like chicken.

She prefers white wine.

She can't eat sweets.

Mr Harris

He doesn't like rice.

He likes red meat and vegetables.

He loves sweets!

He prefers red wine.

Menu

mushroom soup

filet mignon

salmon fillet

green salad

saffron rice

roast chicken

pasta primavera

strawberry sorbet

black forest cake

fresh, steamed vegetables

red or white wine

coffee or tea

Vocabulary   Practical activities
Grammar   Present perfect for experience
Language to go   Asking people about their practical experience

The big adventurer

Aim

To practise using the present perfect (*Have you ever …?*)

Materials

Copies of the gameboard, dice, and counters (something for students to move along the gameboard)

Time

25+ minutes

Preparation

Photocopy the gameboard.

Procedure

1 This activity is a board game. Separate students into small groups of three or four students. Give the groups one copy of the gameboard (you may want to enlarge it on a photocopier), a dice and one coloured counter for each student.

2 Tell students to put their counter on 'Start'. Tell them to take turns rolling the dice. They must then read the question. Example: *Have you ever been to China?* If they HAVE been to China, they stay on that space. If they HAVE NOT, they must go back to the space they started from.

3 Make sure to use the structure in the book: *Yes, I have been to China. No, I haven't been to China.* (The book does not introduce *never* yet, so try to avoid it.)

4 The game is finished when the first student in the group reaches 'Finish'. If they finish too quickly, tell them to play the game again.

The BIG Adventurer

Start

Have you ever travelled to China?

Have you ever eaten sushi?

Have you ever gone scuba diving?

Have you ever seen a famous person?

Have you ever crashed a car?

Have you ever visited a zoo?

Have you ever lived abroad?

Have you ever made a cake?

Have you ever played hockey?

Have you ever eaten tacos?

Have you ever played tennis?

Have you ever worked in a restaurant?

Have you ever had a pet?

Have you ever made a garden?

Have you ever written a letter in English?

Have you ever touched a gun?

Have you ever been to India?

Have you ever used a scanner?

Have you ever seen a shark?

Have you ever been hang-gliding?

Finish

© *Pearson Education 2002*

Vocabulary Activities at work
Grammar *Have to/don't have to*
Language to go Describing jobs

Job descriptions

Aim

Written exercise to practise modals

Materials

One copy of the worksheet for each student

Time

20+ minutes

Preparation

Photocopy the worksheet.

Procedure

1 Hand out the worksheets. The students can do the first part on their own or in pairs. At the top of the page are twelve pictures of different jobs. Below this is a list of the jobs. They simply match the correct job with the correct picture. Check to make sure they all have them correct.
2 Use one of the jobs as an example and ask *What does a doctor have to do?* Write the students' suggestions on the board.
3 Next, assign one job to each student. Tell them to keep it secret. Students then write out a short job description for their assigned job, using *has to*.
4 Check to make sure they've written enough information, then separate students into small groups. Tell students to take turns reading out their job description while their partners try to guess which job it is.

Extension

You could ask students to write down their own job descriptions, or if they are a student, what they have to do for their studies.
When they've finished, collect the descriptions and read them out. Ask students to guess which description belongs to which person.

ANSWER KEY
1 architect   2 pilot   3 hostess   4 designer
5 computer programmer   6 nurse   7 farmer   8 secretary
9 babysitter   10 police officer   11 mechanic   12 doctor

Look at the pictures. Match the name of the job with the correct picture.

____ farmer   ____ architect   ____ secretary   ____ babysitter   ____ police officer

____ designer   ____ pilot   ____ mechanic   ____ computer programmer

____ doctor   ____ nurse   ____ hostess

JOB DESCRIPTION:
Write a description for the job your teacher gives you. What do you have to do?
What DON'T you have to do?

_____

_____

_____

_____

JOB DESCRIPTION:
Write a description of your job/studies. What do you have to do?/What DON'T you have to do?

_____

_____

_____

_____

Vocabulary Parts of the body; illnesses
Function Making and accepting apologies
Language to go Making excuses

Sorry!

Aim

To practise the parts of the body, illnesses and language for making and accepting excuses

Materials

One copy of the board game per four students and one copy of the cut-up cards per four students
Counters and a coin

Time

30 minutes

Preparation

Photocopy the board game. Separate the illness cards and cut them up, one set per group of four.

Procedure

1 Brainstorm illnesses by miming some symptoms. For example, sneeze, hold your head, cough.
2 Divide the students into groups of four. Give each group the board game and a set of the cut-up illness cards. Tell the students to put the cards face down on the square in the middle of the board.
3 Tell students to take a coin and put a counter on 'Start'. Demonstrate heads and tails with the coin. Tell the students they must move from the start to the finish. Student A throws the coin and moves forward one space for heads and two for tails. When he/she lands on a square, Student A must pick up a Truth or Lie illness card and make an excuse, e.g. *I'm afraid I can't come to work today because I've got a cold.* The other students must decide if the excuse is the truth or a lie. If students guess correctly, Student A goes back one and if they do not, Student A goes forward one and stops. When a student throws the coin and lands on a 'You're lying square', they must move back or forward two spaces. Their turn is then over and the next player throws the coin. Tell the students to shuffle the illness cards and start again if they go through them before the end of the game.
4 Demonstrate the activity with one group of students.
5 Monitor the students and make a note of errors.
6 Hold class feedback by picking an illness card and a place and eliciting excuses from the students. Give students feedback on the language errors you noted in stage 5.

Extension

Tell students to write and then roleplay the conversations which take place when the person who made the excuse next sees the person they made the excuse to, e.g. your boss when you return to work after your cold. Students can choose different situations from the game.

START / FINISH	Cinema	Work	You're lying and someone sees you. Go back two spaces	Party
English class				Business meeting
Dinner with your girl/boyfriend's parents		**Truth or Lie**		Weekend in the country
You're lying but no one sees you. Go forward two spaces				You're lying but no one sees you. Go forward two spaces
Drive your friend to the airport	Dinner at your friend's house	You're lying and someone sees you. Go back two spaces	Theatre	Football match

Tell a lie!	**Tell the truth**	**Tell a lie!**	**Tell the truth**	**Tell a lie!**
You want to watch a football match.		You want to watch a programme on TV.		You want to go shopping.

Tell the truth	**Tell a lie!**	**Tell the truth**	**Tell a lie!**	**Tell the truth**
	You want to stay in bed.		You want to be alone.	

Tell a lie!	**Tell the truth**	**Tell a lie!**	**Tell the truth**	**Tell a lie!**
You want to play a computer game.		You want to go to a concert.		You want to surf the Internet.

Vocabulary World issues
Grammar *Will* for predictions
Language to go Making predictions

Future predictions

Aim

To practise *will* and *won't* for future predictions

Materials

One worksheet per group of three plus one cut-up prediction statement per student

Time

30 minutes

Preparation

Photocopy the worksheet (one for each group of three students).

Procedure

1 Set the scene. Ask students to tell you what year it is and what year it will be in 5, 25 and 75 years' time. Brainstorm possible future predictions for these dates. These predictions could be personal to the students or be more general.
2 Give each student a beginning and an ending. Tell them that they do not match. Then ask the students to remember the two halves they have. Tell students they need to find the ending to their beginning to make a future prediction.
3 Demonstrate the activity. Tell students to stand up and mingle, saying their sentences so they can listen and decide if it is the correct ending. When they find the correct ending, tell them to tear their prediction in half and take the paper from the student. Make sure the students remember their statements so they do not read them during the mingling. This will ensure they do the activity orally.
4 Hold class feedback and check all students have the correct predictions.
5 Divide the students into groups of three. Give the students the worksheet with the correct statements and the table. Tell students to decide together which predictions they think will happen in the next 5, 25 or 75 years or never.
6 Hold class feedback. Ask each group to report its predictions and decide as a whole class.

Extension

Give students categories and tell them to brainstorm more predictions for the same time periods, for example, sport, politics, economy etc.

ANSWERS
People will live longer and will die at 150 years old.
Mega cities like Tokyo and São Paulo will get bigger and have 25 million inhabitants each.
We will develop new communications technology to communicate with people from another planet.
Water will become more expensive than petrol.
The sun will become 5 degrees hotter; the temperature change means we will stop going to the beach.
Chinese will become the new world language.
The sea will rise and water will cover Rio, Sydney and New York.
An illness like flu will kill a billion people around the world.
The different states in the USA will become independent countries.

People will live longer	a billion people around the world.
Mega cities like Tokyo and São Paulo will get bigger	to communicate with people from another planet.
Water will become	and have 25 million inhabitants each.
We will develop new communications technology	more expensive than petrol.
The sun will become 5 degrees hotter;	become independent countries.
Chinese will become	and will die at 150 years old.
The sea will rise	will have computers in our body.
The different states in the USA will	the new world language.
An illness like flu will kill	and water will cover Rio, Sydney and New York.
Computers will become so small we	the temperature change means we will stop going to the beach.

In the next 5 years	In the next 25 years	In the next 75 years	Never

Vocabulary   Expressions of time with *for* and *since*
Grammar   Present perfect: how *long/for/since*
Language to go   Talking about how long people do things for

How long have you ...?

Aim

To practise present perfect for unfinished past and *for* and *since*; asking and answering *how long* ... questions

Materials

One copy of the worksheet per student

Time

30 minutes

Preparation

Photocopy the worksheet.

Procedure

1 Tell the students how long you have had various objects, for example, your shoes, your hairstyle, your job. Ask students to decide if what you say is true or false about you. Check students can use *for* and *since* correctly.
2 Give students the photocopy and tell them they need a pen and a book to lean on.
3 Ask students to read the first statement and decide if they think it is true or false about the class. Repeat for the second statement.
Tell students they are going to choose two questions and interview the class to see if the statements are true or false.
4 Elicit the question *How long have you ...?* and check students can pronounce it correctly.
5 Tell students to choose the two questions they want to ask. Alternatively, you could nominate which students ask which questions. The students then stand up and mingle, asking *How long* questions about the two questions they have chosen. Tell students to make a note of how many people answer *yes* or *no* to each statement. (If you have a large class, divide the students into groups of about five.)
6 Hold class feedback. Ask students which statements were true about the class.

Extension

Students work in pairs and interview their partner in more detail about the question which interested them most. For example: *You have had a dog for five years. What is his/her name? What type of dog?*

How long have you … ?

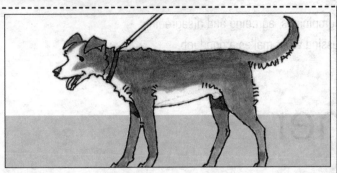

Three people have had a pet for more than a year.

Four people have had a car since 2001.

Four people have been married/in a relationship for more than two years.

Three people have known their best friend since elementary school.

Two people have lived in the same house all their life.

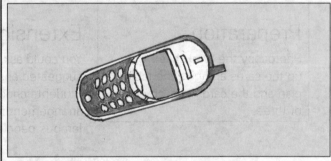

Five people have used a cellphone for more than five years.

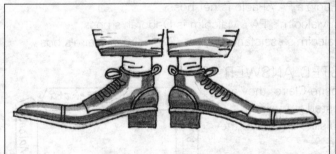

Three people have worn the same pair of shoes all day.

Two people have had the same hairstyle since they were at school.

Five people have studied English for two years.

Five people have used the same bank for more than ten years.

© *Pearson Education 2002*

Vocabulary   Work
Function   Giving opinions, agreeing and disagreeing
Language to go   Discussing what makes a good job

Business dinner

Aim

To practise language for asking / giving opinions and agreeing and disagreeing

Materials

One copy of the worksheet per group of three

Time

30 minutes

Preparation

Photocopy the worksheet. Cut up the cards and give the table plan and the cards to each group of three.

Procedure

1 Set the scene. Tell students that a UK businessman has invited an Italian client to dinner in order to do business together. However, he does not know where to put the different people he has invited.
2 Divide the students into groups of three and give them the dinner table plan and the cut-up cards.
3 Tell the students to answer the question above the table plan by reading the information about the people.
4 Show the students the empty place names on the dinner table plan and ask them to discuss the seating plan and decide who sits next to who.
5 Hold class feedback. Invite suggestions from the different groups and get the whole class to agree on one seating arrangement.

Extension

You could ask the students to discuss the pros and cons of the suggested answer compared to their own.
Students choose six famous people and decide on the best seating arrangement for them. Alternatively, the teacher could provide six famous people they think the students will know.

ANSWER KEY

Malcolm is Eva's husband / Eva is Malcolm's wife.
Renata is Paolo's PA / Paolo is her boss.
Deborah is Malcolm's PA / Malcolm is Deborah's boss.
Claire is Malcolm's assistant director / Malcolm is Claire's boss.

SUGGESTED ANSWER

Paolo opposite Claire: they are both interested in business, like films, dislike sport and they both smoke.

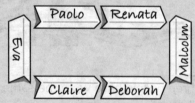

Claire next to Deborah: they are both single, like music and films, and are smokers and vegetarians.
Deborah next to Malcolm: Deborah is Malcolm's PA; they dislike gardening and Deborah can speak Italian.
Malcolm next to Renata: they are non-smokers; Renata speaks good English and they like travelling and both have children.
Renata next to Paolo. She is his PA, speaks good English and they both dislike sport and enjoy gardening.
Eva next to Paolo: Eva can speak Italian; they like gardening, dislike sport and travel and they are similar ages.
Eva next to Claire: They both dislike sport. Claire can talk business to Paolo while Eva can chat more socially.

Business dinner

Name: Paolo di Cannio
Age: 54
Status: single
Job: Director of company
Likes: gardening, films
Dislikes: sport, travelling
Other: speaks a little English, smoker, non-vegetarian

Name: Deborah Fields
Age: 26
Status: single
Job: PA to Malcolm Hyde
Likes: films, music
Dislikes: travelling, gardening
Other: vegetarian, speaks Italian, smoker

Name: Malcolm Hyde
Age: 48
Status: married, two children
Job: Director
Likes: sport, travelling
Dislikes: gardening, films
Other: non-smoker, speaks no Italian, non-vegetarian

Name: Claire Brent
Age: 31
Status: single
Job: Assistant Director
Likes: music, films
Dislikes: cooking, sport
Other: speaks a little Italian, smoker, vegetarian

Name: Eva Hyde
Age: 47
Status: married to Malcolm, two children
Job: Housewife
Likes: cooking, gardening
Dislikes: sport, travelling
Other: non-smoker, speaks Italian, non-vegetarian

Name: Renata Zola
Age: 30
Status: married, one child
Job: PA to Paolo
Likes: travelling, gardening
Dislikes: music, sport
Other: speaks good English, non-smoker, non-vegetarian

What is the relationship between: Malcolm and Eva, Paolo and Renata, Deborah and Malcolm, Claire and Malcolm?

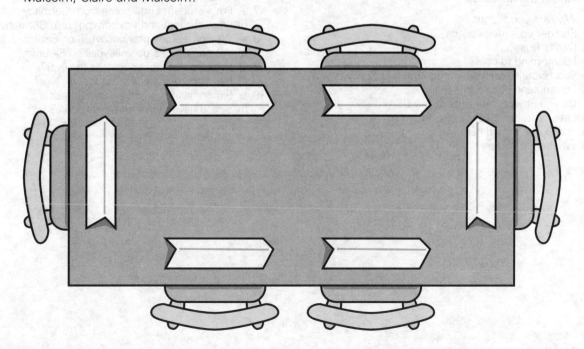

© *Pearson Education 2002*

Test 1

Grammar

1 Circle the correct answers.

1 What's your name?   a) I don't know.
b) John.
c) How are you?

2 Nice to meet you.   a) And you.
b) Yes, it is.
c) You are nice.

3 What's your job?   a) It's a teacher.
b) I'm a teacher.
c) It's good.

4 How are you?   a) Nice to meet you.
b) Yes, I do.
c) Fine, thanks.

5 Are you married?   a) Yes, please.
b) No, I'm single.
c) Yes, I'm fine.

5

2 Use the notes to make conversations. Write full sentences.

1 A: Hi / my / name / Paolo. / I / Italian / and / I / a student.
B: Hi / Paolo. / Nice / meet / you. / I / Sandrine. / I / come / France.

2 A: My / name / Magda. / I / Polish. / your / name?
B: I / John. / I / 28 / and / I / live / Cambridge.

3 A: This / Sandrine. / She / French / and / she / interested / music.
B: Hi. / How / you? / I / like / cook / and / I / love / watch / movies.

4 A: you / married / or / single? / I / married / and / I / have / daughter.
B: I / not / married. / I / live / my parents.

5 A: I / go / swim / every day. / you / like / sports?
B: No. / I / enjoy / sing / and / I like / read.

10

3 Correct the mistakes.

1 Who are you friends?
2 She get up early every day.
3 Ivan is Russia.
4 I don't mind to cook.
5 Sue favourite television programme is *Survivor*.
6 I often send photos in e-mail.
7 Do you have some maps of the USA?
8 Let's order the books in the Internet.
9 Judith don't mind hard work.
10 What are a battery?

10

4 Read the text. Look at the questions and answer *True* or *False*.

I'm a chef in a busy restaurant in Sydney, Australia. My name's Bradley. Every day, I get up early to go to the market. I buy fresh fish, vegetables and meat. At seven o'clock, I walk to the restaurant and I write the menu for the day. I usually drink a cup of coffee with my boss, then we start work. Ten people work in the kitchen with me. I don't like cooking vegetables, so one of the junior chefs does it. I don't mind cooking fish, but I hate cooking meat. I spend many hours a day at work. I usually go home at one o'clock in the morning. Luckily, I'm single so it's OK that I'm often home late.

	True	False
1 The name of the restaurant is Bradley.	☐	☐
2 He gets up early in the morning.	☐	☐
3 He goes to the restaurant by car.	☐	☐
4 His boss drinks coffee, but he doesn't.	☐	☐
5 His favourite job is cooking vegetables.	☐	☐
6 The junior chef cooks all the vegetables.	☐	☐
7 He doesn't like cooking meat.	☐	☐
8 He doesn't work long hours.	☐	☐
9 He often goes home late at night.	☐	☐
10 He's married.	☐	☐

10

5 Tick (✓) the correct sentence in each pair.

1 a) Jill and Keith collects old books.   ☐
b) Jill and Keith collect old books.   ☐

2 a) We go skiing in the Alps every year.   ☐
b) We do skiing in the Alps every year.   ☐

3 a) Has you got a brother or sister?   ☐
b) Have you got a brother or sister?   ☐

4 a) They are good dictionarys.   ☐
b) They are good dictionaries.   ☐

5 a) Bill is businessman.   ☐
b) Bill is a businessman.   ☐

6 a) What are your phone number?   ☐
b) What is your phone number?   ☐

7 a) I'm a student and I come from Germany.   ☐
b) I'm a student and I'm coming from Germany.   ☐

8 a) We sometimes play volleyball on Saturday.   ☐
b) We sometimes go volleyball on Saturday.   ☐

9 a) Have you got these watchs in silver?   ☐
b) Have you got these watches in silver?   ☐

10 a) Simon hasn't got an e-mail address.   ☐
b) Simon haven't got an e-mail address.   ☐

10

Vocabulary

6 Underline the correct options.

1 John loves *wearing / drinking* fresh orange juice.
2 We always *find / have* lunch at one o'clock.
3 Do you like *visiting / going* your friends?
4 I don't like *travelling / visiting* by plane.
5 She never *drinks / wears* that red dress.
6 I often *watch / read* a book in bed.
7 We *play / give* games with the children.
8 He hates *watching / playing* TV.
9 Can you *give / have* me some money?
10 Do you *travel / go to bed* early?

☐ 10

7 Read the text and fill in the form.

Jasmin Salguiero is from Argentina. She lives at 112 Mountbatten Road, London, WR12 8DQ. She studies Modern Languages at University College, London. She wants to travel round Europe from June to September. She's twenty-three.

Name	(1) _____
Surname	(2) _____
Age	(3) _____
Address	(4) _____
Postcode	(5) _____
Place of study	(6) _____
Subject	(7) _____
Travel dates	from (8) _____
	to (9) _____
Nationality	(10) _____

☐ 10

8 Your holiday in India starts next week. Choose a word from the box for each sentence.

sunglasses   alarm clock   phrasebook
walking boots   guide book   umbrella   map
swimming trunks   sweater   camera

1 It's very sunny in India. Be careful of your eyes.
_____
2 You want to take lots of photos.
_____
3 You don't speak any of the Indian languages.
_____
4 You like swimming.
_____
5 You need to get up early to go on sightseeing trips.
_____
6 You don't know how to get from Agra to Jaipur.
_____
7 You want to learn about Indian history and culture.
_____
8 You like walking.
_____
9 Sometimes it rains very hard in India.
_____
10 Sometimes it's cold in the evening.
_____

☐ 10

9 Choose a category (A–E) for each sentence (1–10).

A Talking about sports
B Meeting people
C Talking about collecting things
D Going shopping
E Talking about special occasions

1 Can I try this on, please?
2 We usually have a nice meal on my mum's birthday.
3 Sarah does aerobics once a week.
4 Hi, I'm Mehmet. I'm Turkish.
5 My family celebrates Thanksgiving every year.
6 Have you got a photo collection?
7 Tom goes jogging.
8 How are you? My name's Sally. I'm a teacher.
9 How much are these black trousers?
10 They've got 500 postcards from all over the world.

1 _____ 2 _____ 3 _____ 4 _____ 5 _____
6 _____ 7 _____ 8 _____ 9 _____ 10 _____

☐ 10

10 Tick (✓) the correct options.

1 Which sentence is correct?
  a) I don't like playing basketball. ☐
  b) I don't like play basketball. ☐
2 A calculator is:
  a) an object. ☐
  b) a person. ☐
3 Do you dance:
  a) to music? ☐
  b) with music? ☐
4 Do you travel:
  a) by car? ☐
  b) in car? ☐
5 What do you take to work:
  a) a suitcase? ☐
  b) a briefcase? ☐
6 If you come from Ireland, you are:
  a) Irelandish. ☐
  b) Irish. ☐
7 Which sentence is correct?
  a) This is David's mobile phone. ☐
  b) This is the mobile phone of David. ☐
8 Which sentence is correct?
  a) Have you got this shirt in green? ☐
  b) Have you got this shirt green? ☐
9 Do you say:
  a) a trousers? ☐
  b) some trousers? ☐
10 Which sentence is correct?
  a) This is Peter Brooks and this is her wife, Jane. ☐
  b) This is Peter Brooks and this is his wife, Jane. ☐

☐ 10
☐ 95

Grammar

1 Match the sentences to make conversations.

1 Are you ready to order?
2 Can you speak Italian?
3 What movie did you watch last night?
4 Louise married Tom.
5 Why are you laughing?
6 How much does a mobile phone cost?
7 I usually play golf on Sunday.
8 Can I have a large orange juice, please?
9 Who did you go on holiday with?
10 What was your favourite possession when you were ten?

a) My bike, I think.
b) Yes, and they've got three children now.
c) Because I'm happy.
d) About £100.
e) Yes, I'll have a coffee and a tuna sandwich.
f) Do you? I sometimes play it too.
g) No, but I'm good at French.
h) Yes, of course. Here you are.
i) My friend Tony.
j) It was a comedy about two brothers.

1 _____ 2 _____ 3 _____ 4 _____ 5 _____
6 _____ 7 _____ 8 _____ 9 _____ 10 _____

[10]

2 Underline the correct options.

1 A: I think your book is *on* / *in* the table.
   B: That's strange. I *leave* / *left* it on the bed.
2 A: Can *you* / *I* take your order?
   B: Yes. *I can* / *Can I* have a coke, please?
3 A: How *much* / *many* languages can you speak?
   B: Two. I *study* / *studied* French when I was a child.
4 A: What's Jason *doing* / *do* now?
   B: I think he *watches* / *is watching* the football.
5 A: I *finish* / *finished* work at lunchtime yesterday.
   B: Really? *What* / *Which* did you do in the afternoon?

[10]

3 Find and correct the mistakes. Be careful – there are sixteen sentences, but only ten mistakes.

(1) I went to Greece for my holiday last year. (2) My friend Sally comes too. (3) We stayed on a small island. (4) There is many nice, quiet beaches and a lot of big hotels.
(5) Every day, we went shopping in the market. (6) We bought fresh fish and vegetables and we cooked them on a barbecue.
(7) There were a lot of nice restaurants, but they was quite expensive. (8) The best restaurant was opposite from the bank. (9) It served wonderful Greek salads. (10) We had a car, so we go to see some villages in the mountains.
(11) We meeted a very nice family. (12) They invited us for a meal in his house. (13) We took a lot of photos of their children and we swam in their pool. (14) Sally can speak some Greek, but I can. (15) It were a great holiday.
(16) I want to go back soon.

[10]

4 Choose the correct options to complete the text.

The Boswood family live in New York. They have very busy lives. At the moment, Mr Boswood (1) _____ on a report for an important meeting, and his wife, Sarah, (2) _____ the two youngest children to school.

Peter is the oldest boy. He's at college. He (3) _____ very hard because the final exam is tomorrow. His sister, Liz, also (4) _____ to college, but she (5) _____ last year. Now she (6) _____ for an advertising agency in Boston. She (7) _____ with her husband, Lawrence. This weekend, they (8) _____ with Liz's parents. When they come to stay, the whole family (9) _____ the children out for a day. Last weekend, they (10) _____ to Central Park.

1 a) worked   b) works   c) is working
2 a) took   b) is taking   c) takes
3 a) studied   b) studies   c) is studying
4 a) went   b) is going   c) goes
5 a) leaves   b) is leaving c) left
6 a) working   b) worked   c) works
7 a) lives   b) lived   c) living
8 a) stay   b) can stay   c) are staying
9 a) took   b) is taking   c) takes
10 a) went   b) are going   c) go

[10]

5 Complete the dialogue. Use the correct question words (*who, what, where, when, why, how*) where necessary and the correct form of the verbs in brackets.

Police officer: (1) _____ (get) this wallet?
Man: In the park. I (2) _____ (find) it.
Police officer: Really? (3) _____ (find) it?
Man: Yesterday afternoon.
Police officer: Yesterday. I see. (4) _____ (be) it?
Man: In a bin.
Police officer: In a bin? So (5) _____ (see) it?
Man: I put some paper in the bin and I saw it there.
Police officer: (6) _____ much money was in it?
Man: Not much. About £10. It belongs to Mrs E.J. Simpson.
Police officer: (7) _____ (know) that?
Man: Because I saw her name on the credit card.
Police officer: And (8) _____ is the credit card now?
Man: I (9) _____ (not know).
Police officer: (10) _____ (not know)?
Man: Because I lost it on my way to the police station.

[10]

Vocabulary

6 Complete the crossword.

(crossword grid)

Across

2 Amy is my cousin – she's my aunt's _____ .
4 That café isn't expensive – it's very _____ .
6 The bank is directly _____ the flower shop.
8 I never work _____ – I always finish at five o'clock.
9 I don't want to cook tonight. Let's get a _____ .

Down

1 That was a great meal! It was _____ .
3 What subject did you study when you were at _____ ?
4 A _____ is very useful if you have a lot of dates to remember.
5 Do we turn left here? Can you look at the _____ ?
   I don't know where we are.
7 Are you going to _____ house ·next year?

(10)

7 Underline the correct words.

1 Do you want tea *with* / *in* milk?
2 This is Mary. She is my *brother* / *sister*.
3 I *always* / *never* get up early. I start work at six in the morning.
4 Jack's coat is in the *bookcase* / *cupboard*.
5 Your mother's brother is your *aunt* / *uncle*.
6 We always order chicken *sandwiches* / *cakes* at Café Coco. They're delicious.
7 *Who* / *Where* is London?
8 I can *design* / *drive* a website.
9 Can you *do* / *play* an instrument?
10 Who were the *players* / *actors* in the movie you watched?

(10)

8 Complete the sentences. Use *next to*, *under*, *in*, *above* or *in front of*.

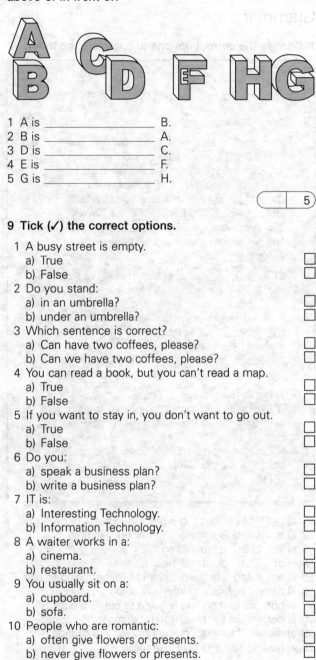

1 A is _____ B.
2 B is _____ A.
3 D is _____ C.
4 E is _____ F.
5 G is _____ H.

(5)

9 Tick (✓) the correct options.

1 A busy street is empty.
   a) True ☐
   b) False ☐
2 Do you stand:
   a) in an umbrella? ☐
   b) under an umbrella? ☐
3 Which sentence is correct?
   a) Can have two coffees, please? ☐
   b) Can we have two coffees, please? ☐
4 You can read a book, but you can't read a map.
   a) True ☐
   b) False ☐
5 If you want to stay in, you don't want to go out.
   a) True ☐
   b) False ☐
6 Do you:
   a) speak a business plan? ☐
   b) write a business plan? ☐
7 IT is:
   a) Interesting Technology. ☐
   b) Information Technology. ☐
8 A waiter works in a:
   a) cinema. ☐
   b) restaurant. ☐
9 You usually sit on a:
   a) cupboard. ☐
   b) sofa. ☐
10 People who are romantic:
   a) often give flowers or presents. ☐
   b) never give flowers or presents. ☐

(10)
(85)

Test 3

Grammar

1 Choose the correct options to complete the letter.

Manchester
3rd July

Dear Jim

I've got lots of exciting news for you.
I (1) _____ married! Françoise is a
lovely person, she's beautiful, intelligent
and very kind. At the moment, she
(2) _____ to be a nurse. Our wedding is
(3) _____ 10 October. It's a Saturday.
The ceremony is (4) _____ two o'clock
in the registry office in Chelsea.
I hope you can come.

I (5) _____ up smoking three months ago
and I feel fantastic. My next plan is to
(6) _____ some weight.
I don't know why, but everybody
(7) _____ on weight when they stop
smoking. I think the
(8) _____ way to get slim again is to
take some exercise, so I'm getting a dog.

When we're married, Françoise and I are
going to (9) _____ house. We want to
get away from the city. But before we do
that,
we are going to go to Turkey. Françoise
thinks I need to (10) _____ more
holidays.

1 a) get   b) can get   c) am going to get   d) getting
2 a) trains   b) is training   c) trained   d) train
3 a) in   b) at   c) to   d) on
4 a) at   b) in   c) on   d) to
5 a) am giving   b) gave   c) give   d) am going to give
6 a) carry   b) find   c) lose   d) stop
7 a) put   b) putting   c) is going to put   d) puts
8 a) better   b) best   c) good   d) most
9 a) move   b) transport   c) remove   d) change
10 a) go   b) see   c) take   d) make

(10)

2 Complete the sentences. Use the words in the box.

| and   an   at   in   on   thousand |

1 _____ Friday, there is a health and safety inspection _____ 10 a.m.
2 We now have two thousand _____ five (2,005) employees.
3 The offices will be closed _____ the weekend.
4 _____ September, there is a meeting of the board.
5 My new company car goes at over 120 km _____ hour.
6 _____ 4 October _____ the evening, there is a staff party.
7 The offices will close _____ the afternoon _____ Christmas Eve.
8 We sold three _____ five hundred copies of the new software last week.
9 The Sydney office opens _____ 8 a.m. _____ Tuesday 2 January.
10 Profits increased _____ 2001.

(10)

3 Make full sentences using the words in brackets.

1 Yesterday / we / not go out / the weather / be / bad
(because)
2 I / love / snow / I / be / frightened of / skiing
(although)
3 Could / you / put / me / through / John / I need / speak / him
(because)
4 I / want / to help / you / I / be / too busy at the moment
(but)
5 It / rain / hard / today / we / going to / stay in
(so)
6 Mary / hate / smoking / she / not give up / till last year
(but)
7 We / be going to / leave / early / tonight / we / not arrive / late
(so)
8 Mark / buy / me / a present / last week / I / tell / him / not to
(although)
9 Could / you / go / to the bank / for me / I / need / money
(because)
10 Johnny / very young / he / can / read and write well
(although)

(10)

4 Underline the correct options.

1 How *much / many* coffee do you drink every day?
2 Do you get *much / many* phone calls at work?
3 I use *a lot of / many* salt in my cooking.
4 How *many / much* time did you spend in Boston?
5 Do your children eat *many / much* chocolate?
6 Are there *much / many* good restaurants in this area?
7 There wasn't *many / much* work to do last week.
8 Do you put *much / many* ketchup on your fries?
9 The firm makes *much / a lot of* money through its website.
10 Do you eat *many / much* bread?

10

5 Underline the correct prepositions of movement.

When you arrive in Stow, turn (1) *left / down* into Park Street. You will see Hamilton's restaurant (2) *past / in front of* you. Go (3) *along / past* the post office and turn (4) *through / into* Sheep Street. Turn (5) *in / right* at the newsagent's and walk (6) *in / along* the street until you see a hotel called The Unicorn. The office is there. Go (7) *up / into* the building and take the lift. Stow Publishing is (8) *in / on* the second floor. Come (9) *to / out of* the lift and come (10) *out / into* the office.

10

6 Complete the sentences using the comparative or superlative form of the adjectives in brackets.

1 A: Can you recommend a good restaurant?
  B: Yes. Go to Zakky's. It's the _____ in town. (good)
2 A: How much money do I need to take on holiday?
  B: Not much, really. France is much _____ than England. (cheap)
3 A: Where can I go climbing?
  B: Go to Mont Blanc. It's the _____ mountain in Europe. (high)
4 A: This shopping centre is very crowded.
  B: Yes, I know. It's the _____ in the whole area. (busy)
5 A: Do you think the weather's good in New York?
  B: Not at this time of year, no. It's _____ than it is here. (cold)
6 A: The boss doesn't like the hotel he stayed in last month.
  B: Oh, dear. I can't book another one. The others are _____ (bad).
7 It rained all through our holiday. Next year we're going to go somewhere much _____ . (sunny)
8 A: Francis was born on the 31 December.
  B: What a great birthday! That's definitely the _____ day of the year. (good)
9 Could you please pass me some water quickly? I think I ordered the _____ curry on the menu. (hot)
10 Look at these baby birds! I think they're the _____ animals I've ever seen! (ugly)

10

Vocabulary

7 Use the words in the box to complete the dialogues.

toilets pool reception gift shop corridor restaurant lift bar first floor basement

1 A: We want to have a drink before dinner.
  B: Certainly, sir. Please go to the _____ . It opens at six o'clock.
2 A: It's very hot. I need a swim.
  B: We have a _____ on the top floor.
3 A: I'm Miss Hancock. I have a reservation.
  B: Welcome to the hotel. Please check in at _____ .
4 A: Could you tell me where my room is?
  B: Yes, of course. It's on the _____ , next to the lifts.
5 A: I'm hungry. Where can I have something to eat?
  B: We serve snacks in the coffee shop or you can go to the _____ .
6 A: I have a car outside. Where can I park it?
  B: Our car park is in the _____ , under the hotel.
7 A: Where are the _____ , please?
  B: The men's are here on the left, and the ladies' are just next to the hotel shop.
8 A: How do I get to the coffee shop?
  B: Go along the _____ and turn right.
9 A: I pushed the button, but nothing happened.
  B: Sorry, madam, I'm afraid the _____ isn't working at the moment.
10 A: We want to buy some stamps and postcards.
  B: The _____ is open all day from 8 a.m. to midnight.

10

8 'Translate' the words in *italics* into American English.

1 We went to the *cinema* last night.
2 The *car park* was very cheap.
3 Let's take the *lift* not the stairs.
4 Do you know where the *toilet* is?
5 The bar is on the *ground floor*.

5

9 Correct the mistakes.

1 How fastly is your car?
2 I can't drink this but it's too hot.
3 Liz going to take more exercise.
4 Wintery is my favourite season.
5 'Can I speak to Phil?' 'Sorry, he not here.'
6 Switzerland is a very mountain area.
7 A whale is the heavier animal in the world.
8 I borrow your mobile, please?
9 Please ask Steve to call back me.
10 Oh, no, look! It snows again!

10

85

Test 4

Grammar

1 <u>Underline</u> the correct options.

1 A: Good evening, may I take your order?
   B: Yes. We *like* / *would like* grilled chicken, please.
2 A: Shall we *go out* / *going out* this afternoon?
   B: OK. Let's go to the park.
3 A: I'm going to read Sarah's diary.
   B: No! You *should* / *shouldn't* do that.
4 A: I *prefer* / *rather* red wine, how about you?
   B: Actually, I like white more.
5 A: Let's *to buy* / *buy* a new car
   B: Excellent idea!
6 A: What about *renting* / *rent* a video tonight?
   B: OK – what shall we get?
7 A: Do you think we *should* / *should to* visit Sam in hospital?
   B: Yes, I'm sure she'd like that.
8 A: I'm going to get a drink. Do you want one?
   B: David *would like* / *likes* a coffee and I'll have some juice.
9 A: Which *you rather* / *would you rather* have – a car or a motorbike?
   B: A motorbike. They're more exciting.
10 A: How about *to play* / *playing* tennis?
   B: Yes, that's a good idea.

                                                                      10

2 Expand the notes to make the questions and answers in this interview. Write full sentences.

1 A: How long / you / be / an actor?
   B: I / 24.
2 A: How long / you / live / in California?
   B: Ten years.
3 A: Why / you / move / here?
   B: I / love / sea.
4 A: How many / movies / you / make / so far?
   B: I / make / fifteen movies.
5 A: When / will / next / film / come out?
   B: Next June.
6 A: You / enjoy / make / your last / movie?
   B: Yes. I / like / do / the / action scenes.
7 A: You / ever / play / romantic roles?
   B: Yes. I / be / romantic hero / in my first movie.
8 A: You / travel a lot / these days?
   B: Yes. Last month / I / go / to Turkey / and / next week / I / fly / to the UK.
9 A: You / ever / go / to the UK / before?
   B: Once. / I / do / a / theatre production / in London.
10 A: What / be / best / thing / you / ever / do?
   B: The best thing / be / when / I / win / an Oscar / in 2000.

                                                                       20

3 Correct the mistakes.

1 Jim said me he saw a really good film last night.
2 Have you been to New Zealand in 2000?
3 What pity you don't feel well.
4 Let's we go and visit Tom and Louise.
5 I haven't drive to work. I can walk because it's close.
6 Sally would rather to sit by the window, if that's OK.
7 Do you think in the future we will to go on holiday in space?
8 I think we don't rent a video tonight.
9 Peter says he can't to come to work today.
10 Jane has been to the shop. She'll be back in a minute.

                                                                    10

4 Complete the second sentences so that they mean the same as the first sentences. Use the correct form of the words in brackets.

1 It is essential to wear a safety helmet while working.
   You _____ while working. (must)
2 Roger started work here a month ago.
   He has _____ a month. (for)
3 Let's buy a new computer.
   How _____ a new computer? (about)
4 I like fish more than meat.
   I _____ meat. (prefer)
5 Patrick told me he was getting married.
   He _____ getting married. (say)
6 It's not necessary for Charlie to wear suits to work.
   Charlie _____ suits to work. (have)
7 What about inviting some friends over tonight?
   _____ some friends over tonight? (shall)
8 Jane said she didn't enjoy the book I lent her.
   She _____ the book I lent her. (tell)
9 Tom is at the office. He went an hour ago.
   He _____ to the office. (go)
10 It would be nice to travel more.
   I _____ to travel more. (like)

                                                                        10

5 Tick (✓) the correct sentences.

1 a) Sue is living in Toronto since 1998.
   b) Sue has lived in Toronto since 1998.
2 a) You don't have to go to work tomorrow.
   b) You mustn't to go to work tomorrow.
3 a) My grandmother played tennis all her life.
   b) My grandmother is playing tennis all her life.
4 a) Did you go to the supermarket yesterday?
   b) Have you gone to the supermarket yesterday?
5 a) I can't come to work. I've got headache.
   b) I can't come to work. I've got a headache.
6 a) No, I disagree with you.
   b) No, I am not agree with you.
7 a) In 2050, people are going to go on holiday in space.
   b) In 2050, people will go on holiday in space.
8 a) I'm going to get a dog. I've always had pets.
   b) I'm going to get a dog. I had always pets.
9 a) Do you have to answer a lot of calls at work?
   b) Do you must answer a lot of calls at work?
10 a) My family have lived in Brussels since 30 years.
   b) My family have lived in Brussels for 30 years.

                                                                        10

Vocabulary

6 Use the words in the box to complete the postcard.

sorry	memorable	knife	scenery	favourite
hours	main	shake	team	fork

Well, here I am in Beijing. My colleagues are great – very friendly and kind, although when I first arrived I had to (1) _____ hands with everyone – it took ages! I work long (2) _____ , but I enjoy it so much that it doesn't matter. Yesterday, I was working with a (3) _____ of engineers. It was a (4) _____ day. We went to see the new factory and had a board meeting, but in the afternoon, they demonstrated all our new products. They are fantastic – you'll be amazed by the technology.

The city is incredible and the (5) _____ all around the area is wonderful. One of my (6) _____ places in Beijing is a little street in the centre where there's a market. I often go to a restaurant there for lunch. We don't use a (7) _____ to cut food or even a (8) _____ . Everyone eats with chopsticks. It was quite difficult for me at first, but I can do it now! They do a great vegetarian noodle dish as a (9) _____ course.

I'm really (10) _____ I haven't written to you before now, but I've just been so busy.

[10]

7 Write the past participle of the verbs to complete the crossword.

Across

6 send	12 work
7 eat	14 write
8 drink	16 live
9 give	17 travel
10 have	18 arrange

Down

1 see	9 go
2 meet	11 dance
3 sing	12 wear
4 study	13 drive
5 be	15 tell

[20]

8 Match the two halves of the sentences.

1 I really loved the special	a) dish?
2 We'd like to order the house	b) idea.
3 James is driving	c) visited Paris?
4 Do you work for an international	d) the phone.
5 I enjoy meeting	e) effects.
6 I'm afraid I	f) clients.
7 Have you ever	g) red, please.
8 Please answer	h) don't feel well.
9 Do you fancy a side	i) to work today.
10 That's a good	j) company?

1 _____ 2 _____ 3 _____ 4 _____ 5 _____
6 _____ 7 _____ 8 _____ 9 _____ 10 _____

[10]

9 Tick (✓) the correct options.

1 The past participle of the verb *see* is *saw*.
  a) True. ☐
  b) False. ☐
2 You give a tip to a:
  a) teacher. ☐
  b) waiter. ☐
3 What other word goes with *knife* and *fork*?
  a) spade ☐
  b) spoon ☐
4 A movie that isn't in colour is called a:
  a) grey movie. ☐
  b) black and white movie. ☐
5 An actress is:
  a) male. ☐
  b) female. ☐
6 Do you work:
  a) in a team? ☐
  b) by a team? ☐
7 Which sentence is correct?
  a) In the future, we all travel in space. ☐
  b) In the future, we'll all travel in space. ☐
8 What is the name for a book you write your personal thoughts in every day?
  a) An agenda. ☐
  b) A diary. ☐
9 Which sentence is correct?
  a) He's been to work. He won't be back till seven. ☐
  b) He's gone to work. He won't be back till seven. ☐
10 In a restaurant, the waiter usually gives you a menu and a wine:
  a) list. ☐
  b) board. ☐

[10]
[110]

143

Tests answer key

Test 1

1 1 b   2 a   3 b   4 c   5 b

2 1 A: Hi, my name's Paolo. I'm Italian and I'm a student.
　　 B: Hi, Paolo. Nice to meet you. I'm Sandrine. I come from France.
　 2 A: My name's Magda. I'm Polish. What's your name?
　　 B: I'm John. I'm 28 and I live in Cambridge.
　 3 A: This is Sandrine. She's French and she's interested in music.
　　 B: Hi. How are you? I like cooking and I love watching movies.
　 4 A: Are you married or single? I'm married and I have a daughter.
　　 B: I'm not married. I live with my parents.
　 5 A: I go swimming every day. Do you like sports?
　　 B: No. I enjoy singing and I like reading.

3 1 Who are ~~you~~ *your* friends?
　 2 She ~~get~~ *gets* up early every day.
　 3 Ivan ~~is Russia~~ is Russian / is from Russia.
　 4 I don't mind ~~to cook~~ *cooking*.
　 5 ~~Sue~~ *Sue's* favourite television programme is *Survivor*.
　 6 I often send photos ~~in~~ *by* e-mail.
　 7 Do you have ~~some~~ *any* maps of the USA?
　 8 Let's order the books ~~in~~ *on* the Internet.
　 9 Judith ~~don't~~ *doesn't* mind hard work.
　 10 What ~~are a battery~~ is a battery / are batteries?

4 1 False (the chef's name is Bradley)   2 True   3 False (he walks to the restaurant)   4 False (he drinks a cup of coffee with his boss)   5 False (he doesn't like cooking vegetables)   6 True   7 True   8 False (he spends many hours at work)   9 True (he usually goes home at 1 am.)   10 False (he's single)

5 1 b   2 a   3 b   4 b   5 b   6 b   7 a   8 a   9 b   10 a

6 1 drinking   2 have   3 visiting   4 travelling   5 wears   6 read   7 play   8 watching   9 give   10 go to bed

7 1 Jasmin   2 Salguiero   3 23   4 112 Mountbatten Road, London   5 WR12 8DQ   6 University College, London   7 Modern Languages   8 June   9 September   10 Argentinian

8 1 sunglasses   2 camera   3 phrasebook   4 swimming trunks   5 alarm clock   6 map   7 guide book   8 walking boots   9 umbrella   10 sweater

9 1 D   2 E   3 A   4 B   5 E   6 C   7 A   8 B   9 D   10 C

10 1 a   2 a   3 a   4 a   5 b   6 b   7 a   8 a   9 b   10 b

Test 2

1 1 e   2 g   3 j   4 b   5 c   6 d   7 f   8 h   9 i   10 a

2 1 on; left   2 I; Can I   3 many; studied   4 doing; is watching   5 finished; What

3 1 *correct*
　 2 My friend Sally ~~comes~~ *came* too.
　 3 *correct*
　 4 There ~~is~~ are / were many nice, quiet beaches and a lot of big hotels.
　 5 *correct*
　 6 We ~~buyed~~ *bought* fresh fish and vegetables and we cooked them on a barbecue.
　 7 There were a lot of nice restaurants, but they ~~was~~ *were* quite expensive.
　 8 The best restaurant was opposite ~~from~~ the bank.
　 9 *correct*
　 10 We had a car, so we ~~go~~ *went* to see some villages in the mountains.
　 11 We ~~meeted~~ *met* a very nice family.
　 12 They invited us for a meal in ~~his~~ *their* house.
　 13 *correct*
　 14 Sally can speak some Greek, but I ~~can~~ *can't*.
　 15 It ~~were~~ *was* a great holiday.
　 16 *correct*

4 1 c   2 b   3 c   4 a   5 c   6 c   7 a   8 c   9 c   10 a

5 1 Where did you get   2 found   3 When did you find   4 Where was   5 how did you see   6 How   7 How do you know   8 where   9 don't know   10 Why don't you know

6 **Across:** 2 daughter   4 cheap   6 opposite   8 late   9 takeaway
　 Down: 1 delicious   3 university   4 calendar   5 map   7 move

7 1 with   2 sister   3 always   4 cupboard   5 uncle   6 sandwiches   7 Where   8 design   9 play   10 actors

8 1 above   2 under   3 in front of   4 in   5 next to

9 1 b   2 b   3 b   4 b   5 a   6 b   7 b   8 b   9 b   10 a

Test 3

1 1 c 2 b 3 d 4 a 5 b 6 c 7 d 8 b 9 a 10 c

2 1 On; at 2 and 3 at 4 In 5 an 6 On; in
7 in; on 8 thousand 9 at; on 10 in

3 1 Yesterday, we didn't go out because the weather
was bad.
2 Although I love snow, I'm frightened of skiing.
3 Could you put me through to John, because I need
to speak to him.
4 I want to help you, but I'm too busy at the moment.
5 It's raining hard today, so we are going to stay in.
6 Mary hates smoking, but she didn't give up till last
year.
7 We're going to leave early tonight so (that) we don't
arrive late.
8 Mark bought me a present last week, although I told
him not to.
9 Could you go to the bank for me because I need
some money.
10 Although Johnny is very young, he can read and
write well.

4 1 much 2 many 3 a lot of 4 much 5 much
6 many 7 much 8 much 9 a lot of 10 much

5 1 left 2 in front of 3 past 4 into 5 right
6 along 7 into 8 on 9 out of 10 into

6 1 best 2 cheaper 3 highest 4 busiest 5 colder
6 worse 7 sunnier 8 best 9 hottest 10 ugliest

7 1 bar 2 pool 3 reception 4 first floor 5 restaurant
6 basement 7 toilets 8 corridor 9 lift 10 gift shop

8 1 movie theater 2 parking lot 3 elevator
4 restroom 5 first floor

9 1 How ~~fastly~~ fast is your car?
2 I can't drink this ~~but~~ because it's too hot.
3 Liz is going to take more exercise.
4 ~~Wintery~~ Winter is my favourite season.
5 'Can I speak to Phil?' 'Sorry, he is not here.'
6 Switzerland is a very ~~mountain~~ mountainous area.
7 A whale is the ~~heavier~~ heaviest animal in the world.
8 Can I borrow your mobile, please?
9 Please ask Steve to call ~~back me~~ me back.
10 Oh, no, look! It ~~snows~~ is snowing again!

Test 4

1 1 would like 2 go out 3 shouldn't 4 prefer
5 buy 6 renting 7 should 8 would like
9 would you rather 10 playing

2 1 A: How long have you been an actor?
B: I've been an actor since I was 24.
2 A: How long have you lived in California?
B: I've lived in California for ten years.
3 A: Why did you move here?
B: I moved here because I love the sea.
4 A: How many movies have you made so far?
B: I've made fifteen movies.
5 A: When will your next film come out?
B: It will come out next June.
6 A: Did you enjoy making your last movie?
B: Yes. I liked doing the action scenes.
7 A: Have you ever played romantic roles?
B: Yes. I was the romantic hero in my first movie.
8 A: Do you travel a lot these days?
B: Yes. Last month, I went to Turkey, and next week
I'm flying to the UK.
9 A: Have you ever been to the UK before?
B: Once. I did a theatre production in London.
10 A: What's the best thing you've ever done?
B: The best thing was when I won an Oscar in 2000.

3 1 Jim ~~said~~ told me he saw a really good film last night.
Jim said ~~me~~ he saw a really good film last night.
2 ~~Have you been~~ Did you go to New Zealand in 2000?
3 What a pity you don't feel well.
4 Let's ~~we~~ go and visit Tom and Louise.
5 I ~~haven't~~ don't (have to) drive to work. I can walk
because it's close.
6 Sally would rather ~~to~~ sit by the window, if that's OK.
7 Do you think in the future we will ~~to~~ go on holiday
in space?
8 I ~~think we don't~~ don't think we'll rent a video
tonight.
9 Peter says he can't ~~to~~ come to work today.
10 Jane has ~~been~~ gone to the shop. She'll be back in
a minute.

4 1 must wear a safety helmet
2 worked here for
3 about buying
4 prefer fish to
5 said (that) he was
6 doesn't have to wear
7 Shall we invite
8 told me she didn't enjoy
9 has gone
10 'd like/would like

5 1 b 2 a 3 a 4 a 5 b 6 a 7 b 8 a 9 a 10 b

6 1 shake 2 hours 3 team 4 memorable 5 scenery
6 favourite 7 knife 8 fork 9 main 10 sorry

7 Across: 6 sent 7 eaten 8 drunk 9 given 10 had
12 worked 14 written 16 lived 17 travelled
18 arranged
Down: 1 seen 2 met 3 sung 4 studied 5 been
9 gone 11 danced 12 worn 13 driven 15 told

8 1 e 2 g 3 i 4 j 5 f 6 h 7 c 8 d 9 a 10 b

9 1 b 2 b 3 b 4 b 5 b 6 a 7 b 8 b 9 b 10 a

145

Forms

> You will sometimes be asked to write in BLOCK CAPITALS so that the form is easy to read.

Title (circle one)	Mr / Mrs / Ms / (Miss)/ other …………
First name	Louise
Surname (BLOCK CAPITALS)	BELL
Address (tick one)	home ✓ work
Street	42 Markham Road
Town/City	Brighton
Region	East Sussex
Country	England
Postcode	BN7 4TY
Phone number	01267 634780
E-mail address	louisebellxx@hotmail.com
Date of birth (DD/MM/YY)	06/07/79
Age	23
Occupation	medical secretary
Nationality	British
Qualifications	B.A. English. Diploma in Secretarial Studies

> Remember to use only important words not sentences:
> *secretary*   ~~I am a~~ *secretary* ✗

Useful language

- Title: *Mr* (man), *Ms* (woman), *Miss* (single woman), *Mrs* (married woman), *Dr* etc.
- Delete (~~Mr / Mrs~~ / Ms / ~~Miss~~)   Tick (Mr ❑ Ms ☑)
  Underline (Mr / <u>Ms</u>)   Circle (Mr / Mrs /(Ms)/ Miss)
- *Surname = Family name*
- *Postcode = Zip code* (USA)
- Date of birth: 06/07/79 = 6th July (UK) or 7th June (US)
  (although here it specifies that the day (D) should come before the month (M))
- *Occupation = job* (it's also acceptable to write *student*)

Teaching notes

1 Brainstorm where and when we fill in forms (registrations, applications, on-line shopping, immigration etc.).
2 Brainstorm the type of information you typically have to give when filling out a form with personal details. Elicit the way that answers are given (i.e. words/notes, not sentences).

3 Go through the model with students.
4 Lessons 2 and 35 in the Students' Book give practice of this kind of writing.

Informal letters

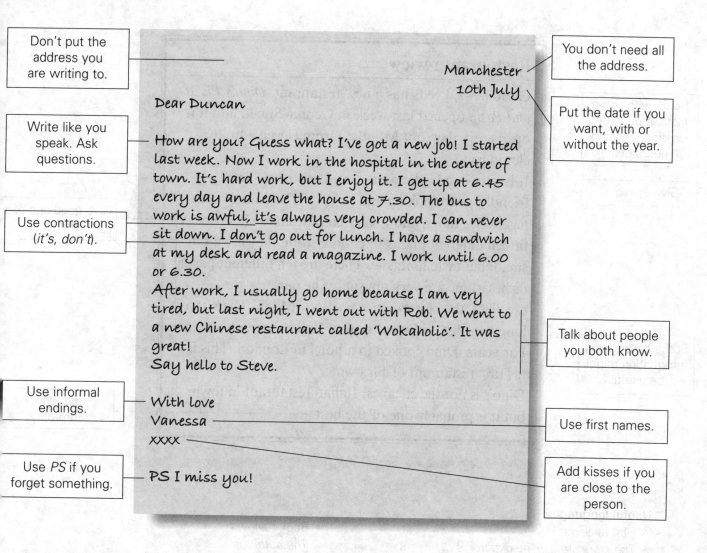

Don't put the address you are writing to.

You don't need all the address.

Put the date if you want, with or without the year.

Manchester
10th July

Dear Duncan

How are you? Guess what? I've got a new job! I started last week. Now I work in the hospital in the centre of town. It's hard work, but I enjoy it. I get up at 6.45 every day and leave the house at 7.30. The bus to work is awful, it's always very crowded. I can never sit down. I don't go out for lunch. I have a sandwich at my desk and read a magazine. I work until 6.00 or 6.30.
After work, I usually go home because I am very tired, but last night, I went out with Rob. We went to a new Chinese restaurant called 'Wokaholic'. It was great!
Say hello to Steve.

With love
Vanessa
xxxx

PS I miss you!

Write like you speak. Ask questions.

Use contractions (it's, don't).

Talk about people you both know.

Use informal endings.

Use first names.

Use PS if you forget something.

Add kisses if you are close to the person.

Useful language
- Letters to thank someone:
  Thanks for your letter.
  Thanks very much for the present.
  I really want to thank you for the great party.
- Letters with news/an announcement:
  Guess what?
  I have some fantastic news!

- Endings:
  love/with love/love from
  (close friends and family)
  best wishes/all the best/take care
  (friends and acquaintances)

Teaching notes
1 Ask students if and when they write letters. Get examples of letters that would be informal (letters to friends/family).
2 Identify how informal letters differ from formal ones (see notes above).

3 Give out the model and ask students to look at the annotated features.
4 Lessons 5 and 19 in the Students' Book give practice of this type of writing.

Restaurant review

Good news, Leeds has a new restaurant. *Dino's Pizza and Pasta* opened last week in George Street, and it is open every day (not Monday) from eleven a.m. to eleven p.m.

It is very good. The waiters and waitresses are friendly, good looking and helpful. The dining room has twelve tables and is very comfortable. There are fifteen different pizzas to choose from; they are a bit small, but taste fantastic. There are ten different pasta dishes, some are very unusual. The desserts are excellent, the best *tiramisu* north of Milan. There is a long wine list and some typical Italian beer.

For years, Dino cooked in a hotel in London. This is his first restaurant of his own.

Dino's is not the cheapest Italian restaurant in town, but it is probably one of the best.

Annotations:

- Begin with some facts, e.g. name, location, opening hours etc.
- Give opinions.
- Some background information might be useful.
- Give good and bad points.
- End with a summary.

Useful language

- Film reviews:
  The stars are ... / The director is ... /
  The film is about ...
  The story takes place in (year / city / country).
  The acting is great / terrible.
  The special effects are ...

- Book reviews:
  The author is ...
  She / He also wrote ...
  The book is about ...
  The main character is ...
  The story takes place in ...

Teaching notes

1 Ask students where they might read reviews (newspapers, magazines, websites etc.) and what is often reviewed (films, plays, concerts, restaurants etc.).

2 Give out the model and ask students to read it, firstly to note what type of review it is (restaurant) and then to find two positive points (staff and desserts) and two negative points (small pizzas and expensive).

3 Draw students' attention to the notes.

4 Lessons 11 and 33 in the Students' Book give practice of this type of writing.

148

Give the story a title to make readers interested.

Use past tenses.

Set the scene – say where and when the story happened.

Introduce people in the story and give some information about them.

A Small World

Fifteen years ago, my best friend <u>was</u> a boy called Jim. He was the same age as me and in the same class at school. He lived in a street near mine. We did everything together. We liked the same things and we enjoyed going to the same places.

One day, my family moved to another town, and I started going to a different school. I didn't see Jim any more, and after a few years, we stopped writing to each other.

After university, I started work in a company. On the first day, the manager introduced me to all the staff. I worked in the same office as Trish. We became very good friends and had fun working together.

At the end of the year, we had an office party. Everyone brought a friend. Trish introduced me to her boyfriend. It was Jim!

Now we are best friends again.

Use time expressions to say when things happened and to put things in order (*then* / *next* / *after that* / *he did A after/before he did B* / *after* / *before doing A, he did B*).

Divide different parts into different paragraphs and put them in a logical order.

Have a good ending – don't just stop.

Useful language
- Beginnings:
  One day ... / Many years ago ...
- Endings:
  Finally ... / In the end ...

Teaching notes
1 Ask students how often they read stories and what type of stories they like.
2 Elicit what is important when telling a story structurally and ways in which a story can be organised (see notes above).

3 Give out the model for students to read. Ask them to identify and give examples of the points in the boxes.
4 Lesson 19 in the Students' Book gives practice of this type of writing.

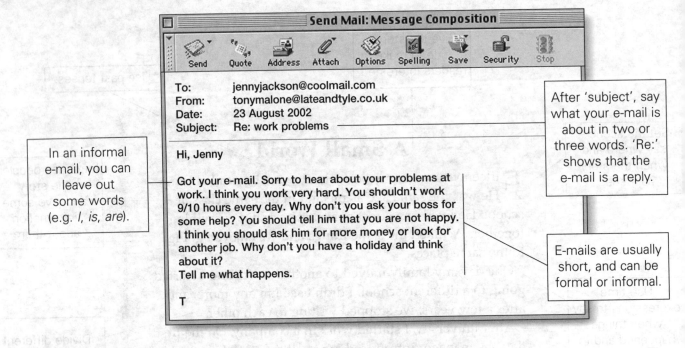

In an informal e-mail, you can leave out some words (e.g. *I*, *is*, *are*).

After 'subject', say what your e-mail is about in two or three words. 'Re:' shows that the e-mail is a reply.

E-mails are usually short, and can be formal or informal.

Within the e-mail image:

Send Mail: Message Composition

Send | Quote | Address | Attach | Options | Spelling | Save | Security | Stop

To: jennyjackson@coolmail.com
From: tonymalone@lateandtyle.co.uk
Date: 23 August 2002
Subject: Re: work problems

Hi, Jenny

Got your e-mail. Sorry to hear about your problems at work. I think you work very hard. You shouldn't work 9/10 hours every day. Why don't you ask your boss for some help? You should tell him that you are not happy. I think you should ask him for more money or look for another job. Why don't you have a holiday and think about it?
Tell me what happens.

T

Useful language

- Beginnings:
  Use *Dear …* if you haven't met the person you are writing to.
  Other informal beginnings are *Hello, John* or just *John*.
- Endings:
  Just your first name or even just your initial.

Teaching notes

1 Ask students how often they use e-mail and who to.
2 Elicit examples of e-mail that would be more formal (e.g. business e-mail, e-mail to people you haven't met), e-mail that would be less formal (e.g. e-mail between colleagues at work) and e-mail that would be very informal (e.g. e-mail to friends and family).

3 Give students the model and ask them to say how formal it is (it's informal). Ask them what they think the relationship is between the writer and the sender (friends) and what the purpose of the e-mail is (giving advice about her work).
4 Lesson 25 in the Students' Book gives practice of this type of writing.

Short notes

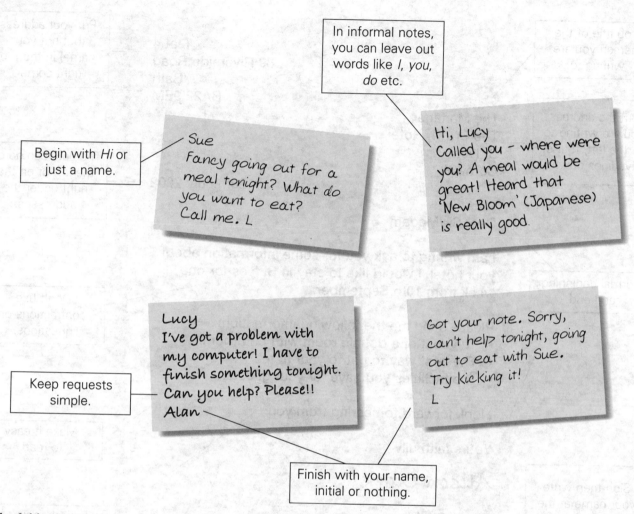

In informal notes, you can leave out words like *I*, *you*, *do* etc.

Begin with *Hi* or just a name.

Sue
Fancy going out for a meal tonight? What do you want to eat?
Call me. L

Hi, Lucy
Called you – where were you? A meal would be great! Heard that 'New Bloom' (Japanese) is really good.

Lucy
I've got a problem with my computer! I have to finish something tonight. Can you help? Please!!
Alan

Got your note. Sorry, can't help tonight, going out to eat with Sue.
Try kicking it!
L

Keep requests simple.

Finish with your name, initial or nothing.

Useful language
- Going out:
  Gone out. Back in 5 mins.
  See you later.
- Phone messages:
  John called – please call him back.
  John called – he says ...
- Reminders:
  Don't forget to ...
  Please remember to ...

Teaching notes

1 Ask students when they write notes (messages, requests, questions, reminders) and who to (colleagues, friends, flatmates, yourself etc.).

2 Elicit style of notes – very informal with reduced sentences using few words.

3 Give them the model and check that they understand that these are two pairs of notes. Ask them to identify the purpose of each pair of notes (invitation with acceptance and request with refusal / suggestion). An alternative is to cut them up and ask students to decide which reply goes with which note.

4 Lesson 27 in the Students' Book gives practice of this type of writing.

Put your address (but not your name) in the top right corner.

Job title of the person you are writing to.

Put the address you are writing to on the left, four or five lines down.

The date can go on the left or on the right under the addresses.

Formal beginning and end.

Don't use contractions or questions.

Make it easy to read.

Typical ending for a formal letter.

Sign then write your name at the bottom of the letter.

Flat 4
89 Riverside Road
Bath
BA22 9EM

The Manager
The Crown Hotel
St Ives
Cornwall

26th July 2002

Dear Sir/Madam

I am writing to ask you for some information about your hotel. I would like to stay in St Ives for one week from 10th September.

Please send me the following information:
- The cost of a double room with bathroom.
- The best way to get to your hotel.
- The facilities you have for your guests.

I look forward to hearing from you.

Yours faithfully

Alison Clark

Alison Clark

Useful language
- Beginnings and endings:
  If you know the name of the person you are writing to, begin *Dear Mr/Ms XXXXX* and end *Yours sincerely*.
  If you don't know the name, begin *Dear Sir/Madam* or *Dear Sir or Madam* and end *Yours faithfully* (UK) or *Yours truly* (US).
- First sentence:
  Application: *I am writing to apply for ...*
  Complaint: *I am writing to complain about ...*
- Final sentence:
  Invitation: *I look forward to meeting you.*

Teaching notes
1 Ask students to think of when they need to write formal letters (applications, requesting information, complaints, formal invitations).
2 Elicit information about layout and organisation.
3 Give out the model for students to read and compare it with information they gave in Step 2. Ask students to compare these conventions with those in their own country.
4 Lesson 35 in the Students' Book gives practice of this type of writing.